THE OMEGA
MANIFESTO

By
Scott Keisler

Unless otherwise identified, Scripture quotations are from the New American Standard Bible. Copyright 1995 by the Lockman Foundation. All emphasis in Biblical quotations is the author's.

Published in the United States of America
For Worldwide Distribution.

ISBN 978-0-615-79910-0

Cover designed by Joseph Fioramonti,
POST MORTAL design

Published and distributed by
ScottKeisler.com

OmegaManifestoBook.com

Email: info@scottkeisler.com

Contents

PAGE

Acknowledgments. 5

Introduction. 7

Chapter 1   True Truth 9

Chapter 2   Fallout 20

Chapter 3   In the Beginning 31

Chapter 4   Bible Prophecy 47

Chapter 5   Israel 66

Chapter 6   The Old World Order 97

Chapter 7   The New World Order. 112

Chapter 8   Eugenics, the Environment, and Beyond 142

Chapter 9   The Church and the NWO. 164

Chapter 10   Days of Noah. 184

The Omega Manifesto. 223

Index 227

About the Author 239

Acknowledgments

I wish to thank Francis Schaeffer, John Loeffler, and Ravi Zacharias for providing the intellectual impetus behind this book. I also want to thank Chuck Missler and Chuck Smith for their theological, prophetic, and pastoral insights.

I am exceedingly indebted to Gary Kah. Thank you, Gary, for taking me seriously and for being so generous in sharing your time and resources with me since 2006. I also want to acknowledge Carl Teichrib, who has kindly taken the time to answer my many questions over the last year or two. Carl's research raises the bar to a standard to which we should all aspire. I would be remiss if I did not also recognize Doug Riggs, who graciously reviewed this manuscript, offering invaluable insight and guidance. Kudos are also in order for Joseph Fioramonti of POST MORTAL design. His exceptional cover design, typesetting, and help with the website—not to mention his strategic advice—have all truly been a God-send.

Thank you also to Dr. Stanley Monteith, who is always quick to respond to my emails despite his crazy schedule. On more than one occasion his unique show, Radio Liberty, has pointed me in the proper direction. Thank you to L. A. Marzulli, whose field research and expertise helped to shape the final chapter of this book, even where not explicitly stated.

I also need to recognize Tom Horn and Russ Dizdar, both of whom have fearlessly tackled radical evil while still managing to be salt and light on the earth (a feat which is more easily said than done).

While the individuals listed above may not endorse everything that I say in this book, I do want to publicly thank each of them for inspiring me to aim high (and up).

Finally, I want to thank my father and mother for snatching me out of the fire and giving me the opportunity to have the life that I have had. Words do not adequately express how much you mean to me. It also turns out that my mother is quite the editor as she ironed out quite a few last minute wrinkles in the manuscript. Awesome job!

And last of all, I dedicate this book to my sister, who has always been my biggest fan and greatest friend.

Introduction

When I lay awake at night and my mind is going at 1,000 mph, usually what's eating at me is the fact the reality is so hardcore, yet so many people seem blissfully unaware. I realize that people nowadays are working harder and harder just to break even—some are working two and three jobs just to pay the bills in the recession recovery that never was. I know people are into their families and their kids, and the thought of history taking a radical turn for the worse is unthinkable. Trust me: I get it.

But that's just the problem. People don't think about the unthinkable. Or if they do, they quickly sweep it under the rug and continue on with their lives as if the way things currently are is the way things will always be. The technical term for this approach to the future is normalcy bias. Yet history shows that there is no reason to assume that the status quo will always prevail.

What if we wake up one day and the world is completely different from the world we have always known?

To make matters worse, we live in a socially engineered society in which truth is either suppressed, politicized, or ignored. The educational establishment and the media have an agenda and much of the "reality" that has been pushed upon us has been filtered through the lens of a phony left-right political paradigm that operates on the basis of a flawed philosophical system. Revolutionaries have literally transformed our culture, yet few people have been taught what has actually happened, how it happened, and why it happened.

Not only does this book answer these questions, *The Omega Manifesto* also points to the who behind it all. As you read through this important work, we will deal with the core issues operating just below the surface of what we perceive as reality—and we will do so on a foundational level. I have labored to write a work that is pragmatic and approachable while trying *not* to be stuffy or overly academic. That said, I haven't employed the lowest common denominator approach either. Portions of *The Omega Manifesto* may be challenging, both in terms of sharpening your worldview and stretching your faith. I have tried to approach the difficult topics that will be encountered over the next ten chapters in a measured way. I have been mostly successful, though there are a couple of classic Scott rants.

If you take this book seriously, by the end you will possess a foundation that will help you to sort fact from fiction and reality from deception in the coming radical global paradigm shift. And that shift may overtake us all sooner rather than later.

What if we wake up one day and the world is completely different from the world we have always known?

Chapter 1—True Truth

There is no debating that our world is as chaotic as it has ever been. In our own times we are witnessing worldwide economic hardships, social upheavals, and color revolutions around the globe. We also see fighting along ethnic, class, and political lines. In the United States the division is so sharp that we have literally seen a complete breakdown in communication as each respective side in the culture war has resorted to lobbing non-productive epithets at the other. It's not that the "other" side has rejected the message. The other side [often] failed to even understand the message.

How did we get here? After all, we didn't arrive at this point in space-time (early in the 21st century) in a vacuum. This chapter will look at the philosophical heart of the culture war. We will examine not *what* each side thinks but *how* it thinks. Once we understand the *how*, the *what* which follows will begin to make much more sense.

Classical Western Thought

We humans are unique in the natural world. There's no getting around it. We are unique because not only do we know, but we *know* that we know. An animal may "know" that it is alive, but that animal has no capacity or ability to analyze its "aliveness." We humans, on the other hand, always seem to be obsessing about our aliveness. This innate ability to explore our own existence is uniquely human.

Historically, humanity's bent towards self-exploration gave rise to epistemology, which is the branch of philosophy concerned with the theory of knowledge—its scope, its limits, how we know, and how we know that we know. Philosophically, if one traces the lineage of Western thought back through the millennia, one finds that two fundamental ideas or presuppositions inevitably emerge:

1) Truth exists
2) Truth is knowable

These presuppositions require qualification. By truth I mean Universal Truth, that is to say, absolute propositions (truth claims) by which all other propositions may be measured or judged.

Truth exists.

The second proposition, that truth is knowable, is important because if we know that Truth exists, but we fail to ascertain or discern what that Truth is, for all intents and purposes— from our human point of view—Truth may as well not exist.

Historically these two fundamental presuppositions (Truth exists, Truth is knowable) undergird the Western intellectual tradition. Building upon this foundation, we arrive at the first rule of classical logic:

A is equal to A, and A is not equal to non-A.

If proposition A is true, then proposition non-A cannot also be true. We can call A our *thesis* and non-A our *antithesis*. Notice that Truth is by its very nature an exclusive entity. There exists an inherent *antithesis* between that which is True and that which is not.

The approach to epistemology we have just outlined is called Didactic thought. Based upon this Didactic methodology, Western Philosophy historically sought out to set forth a unified theory of knowledge—to give an account for the unity in diversity that we observe and experience empirically in the cosmos.

To illustrate, let us examine a famous Renaissance fresco by Raphael called *The School of Athens*.

Many aspects of this interesting painting could be discussed, but for our purposes let us focus our attention on the center of the work. Here the viewer will find two eminent figures from The Academy (The School of Athens), the distinguished Plato and his famed pupil Aristotle. To the left, Plato has his right arm extended vertically, his index finger pointing upward toward the heavens—emphasizing the Platonic focus on the Universal (as in Universal Truth). To Plato's left is Aristotle, whose right hand is extended out in front of him, palm horizontal to the ground—emphasizing the Aristotelian focus on the Particular (that which is diverse). Where Plato started from the Universal in order to talk about the Particular, Aristotle started with the Particular in order to talk about the Universal. Thus we observe a microcosm of the ancient riddle of philosophy: How to set forth a *unified* theory of knowledge while also providing for the *diversity* that we observe and experience in our world.

This is where the word university comes from—unity in diversity. Both Plato and Aristotle assumed that Universals (Absolute Truths) existed though their methodologies and points of emphasis differed.[1]

---

[1] Note: I am not here promoting their philosophical ideas, I am merely pointing out that both men accepted the idea of Universal Truth in the cosmos.

The Academy by Raphael—Plato and Aristotle

Truth exists. Truth is knowable.

The history of philosophy (up to a certain point) can be summed up as a series of attempts to solve this riddle of unity in diversity via movements and subsequent reactionary movements—the latter usually overcompensating for the errors of the former. Some philosophic schools emphasized rationality and some emphasized experience. Some emphasized asceticism while others emphasized indulgence and hedonism. Some emphasized the traditions of the past, some emphasized the happenings of the present, while still others emphasized a utopianist vision of the future. Another common error was to place one aspect of humanity, for example reason, in a position of primacy over the other aspects of humanity, for example experience or context (tradition). The list could go on and on.

But down through the ages these two basic presuppositions (Truth exists, Truth is knowable) and the Didactic methodology (antithesis) remained a constant. From the Classical period and the Academy (which approached philosophy from a pagan point of view), to the rise and decline of the Roman Empire and the Middle Ages (which saw a mix of paganism and Christian thought), through the Renaissance and the Reformation (where a split occurred between the Humanistic and Judea-Christian worldviews), all the way up to the time of the French Revolution and the beginning of the Enlightenment in the 18th century (which posited Humanism absolutely).

Let's take a closer look at this flow of history so that we can better understand how we arrived at where we find ourselves today.

The Humanism of the Renaissance attempted to set out a unified theory of knowledge (unity in diversity) starting from man and from man alone. Humanists like Michelangelo and Leonardo Da Vinci, through their art and mathematics, attempted to construct a Universal (Absolute Truth) out of finite particulars, with man as the only point of reference. This is not to say that many good things didn't happen during the High Renaissance in Southern Europe. This period saw a new emphasis on Classical Greek and Roman literature *(ad fontes)* while writers like Dante wrote their works in the vernacular of the common people. Painters used perspective and even depicted light coming from the proper direction in their landscapes as a new appreciation of nature developed (as opposed to the unintelligible mysticism in the art of the Middle Ages). There were great feats of architecture that combined artistic elegance with profound mathematical understanding. As the saying goes, a Renaissance man was truly a jack of all trades and a master of at least *one* (*not* none).

But the Humanism of the Renaissance failed to come up with Universal Truth starting and ending with man alone. As Francis Schaeffer points out in *How Should We Then Live?*, Da Vinci died in despondency foreseeing where Humanism would end up. Similarly, the Humanistic swagger of Michelangelo's midlife work seems to fade or even disappear by the end of his life.

A few centuries later, the Enlightenment posited man absolutely as the starting point, imagining that man was perfectible while romantically envisioning the soon-coming utopian paradise that enlightened man would create. But the French Revolution was a bloodbath and the folly of romanticized Humanism had to be faced. As John Loeffler of the *Steel on Steel* radio broadcast rightly says, reality always gets to speak last.

Modern Thought

This brings us to the German philosopher G. W. F. Hegel (late 18th, early 19th century). Hegel observed that philosophy (that is, Humanistic Philosophy) had exhausted all conceivable options and had failed to arrive at a unified theory of knowledge. Hegel had two choices. He could have either looked upward, turning to God for his Universal—unthinkable for a Humanist—or he could have tinkered with his epistemological methodology (antithesis). Recall the prevailing methodology up to Hegel:

A is equal to A, A is not equal to non-A

Or said another way:

Thesis—Antithesis

In this Didactic system, when a *thesis* encounters an *antithesis* in the public marketplace of ideas, there may be a moment of conflict upon impact, but in the end *thesis* prevails and *antithesis* is discarded. Why? Because a thesis cannot be simultaneously True and untrue. Hence the term antithesis.

But Hegel had a new idea. Hegel (when boiled down) proposed a triadic structure in place of the dualism of the Didactic. In so doing, Hegel preserved the components of *thesis* and *antithesis*, but he posited a third entity which has been called synthesis. Like so:

Thesis—Antithesis
V
Synthesis

For Hegel, when a *thesis* (A) encounters an *antithesis* (non-A) in the public marketplace of ideas, the two entities act, react, and impact upon each other like before, only instead of *thesis* prevailing and *antithesis* being discarded, a third entity comes into being—a *synthesis*. It is important to catch this. The *thesis* and the *antithesis* have *both* contributed to the new outcome—the *synthesis*. Hegel's system was not so simple and, as Francis Schaeffer pointed out, Hegel himself may not have followed his own idea all the way through to its logical conclusions.

Nonetheless, do you see what has just happened? Hegel has just made truth a *relative* proposition; he has given up on the idea of Universal Truth. If you have to close the book and think about this one for a second, please do, because this is very important. To Hegel, non-A is *just as valid* as A as we pursue truth in the public marketplace of ideas.

But it doesn't stop with relative truth. In Hegel's new methodology, the aforementioned *synthesis* eventually becomes a new *thesis*. Thus another *antithesis* will inevitably come along, acting and impacting upon the new *thesis* and producing another *synthesis*. And so the process continues indefinitely. So for Hegel, not only has truth become a relative proposition, it has also become a *moving target*—truth resides on a constantly pitching deck, as John Loeffler puts it.

This new methodology is known as the Hegelian Dialectic, or the Dialectical process. In the Dialectic, we are dealing with relative, evolving truth. And make no mistake, the implications and ramifications of this new way of thinking reach far beyond the ivory towers of intellectual speculation. We are dealing with the very core of how we approach truth and knowing. As I said at the beginning of the chapter, not *what* we think, but *how* we think. Hegel's methodology (the Dialectical process) is the philosophical lynch-pin of Materialism, Progressivism, Modernism, Post-Modernism, and even Marxism. Contrary to what is commonly taught in public schools these days, the core of Marxism lies neither in its economic ideas, nor in its atheism, the core of Marxism lies in the Hegelian Dialectic.

If Hegel cracked open the door of modern thought, then it was Soren Kierkegaard who swung the door wide open. The Danish Philosopher Soren Kierkegaard (19th century) is the father of Existentialism, both secular and theological. Kierkegaard added a new twist to the Dialectic. Kierkegaard accepted the new methodology of synthesis as outlined above, but he also posited that one could not arrive at this synthesis by way of reason (for example using empirical data). Instead, Kierkegaard said that one arrives at synthesis by way of a non-rational leap of faith. Rationalistic empiricism plays no role in his existential faith experience. The importance of this, once again, cannot be overstated. Think about this carefully. Kierkegaard created a radical dichotomy between faith and reason. In this worldview, faith and science are compartmentalized. So where Hegel made truth a relative proposition and a moving target, Kierkegaard came along and *fragmented* truth. Do you now see why we so often observe an inherent animosity between science and religion in our day? This animosity wasn't always so and it need not be! (More on this later.)

Hegel and Kierkegaard lead us directly to Modern thought and Modern man. We see the influence of their ideas playing out in 21st century culture on a daily basis. On a personal level, we hear people saying things like,

> "Well, you have your truth and I have mine . . . I have my own beliefs about things." (Truth is relative and therefore personal.)

You have probably heard a politician (or a friend) say something like this:

"Well I *personally* believe thus and so is wrong, but who am I to foist my views upon another?"

This way of thinking leads to the inevitable,

"Don't judge me!"

Why? Because to modern man (in the gender inclusive sense of the term), it is arrogant to claim possession of Absolute Truth! Following Hegel truth became personal, following Kierkegaard faith became private. Thus we arrive at the prevailing worldview of our time—relative, evolving, fragmented, personal truth.

True Truth!

Notice that the Humanism of the Renaissance and the Enlightenment, operating on a Didactic base (antithesis) failed. It didn't fail because there is no such thing as Absolute Truth (True Truth as Francis Schaeffer called it). It failed because it is impossible for man to set out a unified theory of knowledge using himself as the only point of reference! As I alluded to earlier, the Humanists could have looked beyond themselves (i.e. to God), but that would have been throwing in the towel on Humanism—for Humanism presupposes that man is his own god, thus implicitly leaving the idea of a supernatural God out of the equation. (At this point I am not even saying *which* God.) In a philosophical workaround, Hegel and Kierkegaard came up with a new methodology— the Dialectical process and a leap of faith![2]

---

[2]Both Hegel and Kierkegaard were Christians, at least in name. But they were expressing their Humanism using a Christian vocabulary. This may sound strange, but theological liberals have always expressed the philosophical spirit of the age in Christian terms.

Yet the Secular Humanism of Modernity and Modern man, operating on a Dialectical base, is in the process of dying right before our eyes. As Western culture comes apart at the seams, politically correct narratives (read cultural Marxism) are also dying. Rays of reality are slowly starting to beam through cracks in the cultural facade. The world cannot operate (for long) on the basis of relative, evolving, fragmented, and personal truth. In the next chapter, we will deal with some of the implications of the reality of Absolute Truth in our world.

This first chapter has established an important foundation for the rest of the book. The first three planks of *The Omega Manifesto* are as follows:

1) Truth exists.
2) Truth is knowable.
3) Approach Truth Didactically (antithesis), not Dialectically (synthesis).

Chapter 2—Fallout

When we talk about Absolute Truth, we are talking about more than merely a set of ideas about which a large number of people agree. As defined in chapter one, Absolute Truths are absolute propositions by which all other propositions may be measured or judged. Mathematics is a good place to start here. When we look at the math problem 3x3, we know the answer is nine. Not eight, not ten, *nine*. When we are dealing with Truth, we are of course dealing in the arena of human knowledge. But if we are in this arena for any length of time at all the conversation will inevitably turn to right and wrong. Truth and morality go hand in hand. It is very difficult to have a conversation about Absolute Truth (Universal Truth) without bringing up morality—without talking about the concept of right and wrong.

The next time you go to a mall or a restaurant or the next time you overhear a conversation at work, notice how often people evoke the idea of right and wrong (especially when they are upset). You'll hear people saying things like,

> "The bank should have let me have my money right then and there, they are so *greedy.*"

Or,

> "It's *not fair* that I always have to work on Saturdays when my boss almost never comes in on the weekend."

But think about it. We seem to take it for granted that greed is a bad thing and that fairness is good. People constantly appeal to this unspoken standard. And we all seem to know about it.

And yet something seems to be amiss! In mathematics, you never hear anybody saying 3x3 *ought to be* nine because 3x3 *is* nine. But in human conversations we hear the word *ought* or *should* come up all the time. It seems that everyone knows what people *ought* to do, and yet nobody seems to be doing what they *ought* to do *all the time*. This unspoken standard, which throughout history has been called Natural Law, seems to originate from outside of humanity. (Why would humans come up with a system of morality that we can never quite seem to keep?) Humanists have attempted to get around this notion of Natural Law by arguing that the standard of right and wrong that everybody seems to know about is a matter of historical and social conditioning. But as C. S. Lewis brilliantly points out in *Mere Christianity*, a soldier on the battlefield would probably *rather* choose cowardice and flee, yet something impels him to choose bravery—even though being brave is not only inconvenient, it is imperiling! In a Materialistic and Humanistic universe, why would mankind feel obliged to choose the weaker of two impulses? If we really live in an impersonal universe in which nobody is at home, and if there really is no Natural Law in the social universe, why on earth would any soldier ever voluntarily *choose* bravery over cowardice?

On the other hand, if there *is* a Natural Law in the universe, then where does that Law come from? We already know that it comes from outside of humanity because we know we aren't keeping it all of the time and yet we feel obliged to try. (Otherwise we would be masochists.) As Lewis again points out, whatever (or whoever) is behind the Law, it seems to be like us, at least in so far as it seems to be conscious, to prefer one thing over another, and to even have purpose. Remember what I said in the first chapter? I said that humans are unique in the natural world because not only do we know, but we *know* that we know—unlike plants or even animals. The *who* behind morality seems to be conscious and sentient like we are.

If There's a Standard . . .

Now let's go on the offensive for a moment here. Perhaps you have noticed that the very people who intellectually hold to the idea of relative, evolving, and personal truth, when confronted with the possibility of the existence of God, will ask—seemingly invariably:

> If God exists and God is really good, then why do
> such evil things happen all the time?

Understand that this is a valid question and a difficult question. But the difficulty is more emotional than it is rational. If one stops to examine the question carefully one will see that the question takes the existence of evil for granted: . . . *Why do evil things happen?* The existence of evil presupposes the existence of good. And the existence of good presupposes a standard by which to differentiate between good and evil. Finally, the existence of a standard of good and evil implies the existence of a standard-giver. Thus the question asked ostensibly to *undermine* the existence of God actually ends up *implying* God's existence.

Are we really willing to live with the implications of a world where the idea of truth and morality are merely relative? As Ravi Zacharias has said, are we really willing to say that Hitler's actions were distasteful, even deviant, but not absolutely immoral? This is not sophistry. These are serious philosophical questions which demand an answer. I believe John Loeffler is correct when he observes that skeptics and humanists are very good at asking the difficult questions, but they do not do so well when it comes to answering these fundamental questions of human existence.

Materialism

Speaking of fundamental questions, and since we are already on the offensive, let's stay on the offensive for a while. Let us deal with Materialism, which is a Humanistic Cosmology. The issue of where mankind comes from is indeed one of the fundamental questions of our existence. The Materialistic wolrdview says that the universe is all there is. The Merriam-Webster dictionary defines Materialism as follows:

> A theory that physical matter is the only or funda-
> mental reality and that all being and processes and
> phenomena can be explained as manifestations or
> results of matter.

Evolutionary theory and Big Bang cosmology are two subsets of the Materialistic worldview. Evolutionary theory says that life spontaneously generated as the result of energy (matter) plus time plus chance.

Many atheistic secularists try to frame the origins debate as science versus religion (for example evolution versus intelligent design). Recall how Kierkegaard's Existentialism fragmented truth and resulted in a radical dichotomy between faith and reason. According to this worldview, science is rational and empirical while faith is intrinsically non-rational. But in a world where Absolute Truth exists, this dichotomy is unnecessary and indeed even illogical! Now watch this brilliant observation that I credit to Ravi Zacharias. For Kierkegaard, meaning is bound up in faith (not reason). But faith according to Existentialism, as we've seen, is non-rational. Think about this for a moment. Do you see how we have arrived at the modern definition of faith—that is, faith *in* faith, which has sometimes even translated to believing in spite of the evidence. But when a Naturalistic scientist scoffs at my Supernaturalistic cosmology as a non-rational fairytale that I hold to like a crutch for comfort and meaning, I must kindly remind him that his empiricism and reason rooted in Naturalistic science must ultimately be meaningless! If he insists upon foisting his radical faith-reason dichotomy upon me, I must insist that he foists it upon himself. If my faith can't include reason, then his reasoning can't ultimately have any meaning—since in his own dichotomy meaning comes down on the side of faith! But who can live like this? Why would anyone want to?

Strictly speaking, the origins question is not inherently a scientific question, it is a philosophical question. The starting point is not directly observable, thus we are forced to speculate. Think of it like this, Materialism (Scientific Naturalism), starts out with the following presupposition:

In the beginning there was nothing, and it exploded.

This is not a cutsie turn of phrase! Materialists hold to their Darwinian dogmas with religious-like fervor. In the 1920s and 30s, the Humanists merely wanted equal time for evolution in the school classrooms that taught creationism. Once this was accomplished, the Humanists later kicked the creationists out of the classroom. Now they scoff at the idea that Intelligent Design should share equal time in the classroom with evolution. (Intelligent Design isn't even the same as Creationism.) Why is it that the Humanists hold themselves to one standard and everybody else to another? Why is it that in the name of tolerance and inclusion they can be so intolerant and exclusive?

Of course we have seen why! Humanistic philosophy pushes relative and evolving truth. Today's truth is tomorrow's synthesis. Is it any wonder that "truth" is used as a political expediency that can be altered at will by the powers that be in our culture—all in the name of "progress"? To this end, G. K. Chesterton rightly asks, if the standard changes, how then can there be improvement, as improvement implies the fixed standard that allegedly doesn't exist?! If we are to operate on a Dialectical basis absolutely, the perfectibility of man must be a meaningless hoax!

And look, I am absolutely *not* opposed to science. I quite enjoyed biology and physics in high school and college. There is certainly no reason to fear science, as some religious types do. In fact, I want to help science be more...well, scientific! Humanistic Darwinism is not only politicizing science (we'll see evidence of this in chapter eight), it is destroying the foundations on which good science should rest—like a man sawing off the very branch on which he sits.

Fallout

Now, let's revisit a statement made in chapter one, where I wrote:

Western Philosophy historically sought out to set forth a unified theory of knowledge—to give an account for the unity in diversity that we observe and experience empirically in the cosmos.

The very word university speaks to this age-old quest. As Ravi Zacharias has pointed out, if we observe unity in diversity in the cosmos—at least to the extent that we discern that unity in diversity is a desirable philosophical goal—then should we not expect to find unity in diversity in the first cause behind the universe (the Cosmological Argument)? Is not this ancient riddle of unity in diversity emphatically resolved in the first cause of the Christian Trinity—one God, one essence, and yet three personages—Father, Son, and Holy Spirit? And isn't it another fantastic coincidence that this Christian God of the Bible speaks of Original Sin, which accounts for the Natural Law that everybody seems to know about, yet nobody seems to be keeping *all* the time? In other words, do you not find it strange that this Triune God seems to be the conscious mind behind Natural Law?

In a more broad sense, how can one look at the universe and not see the fingerprints of God all over the place? As technology explodes and we are better equipped to explore our universe, we have discovered that on a micro level life seems to be irreducibly complex! To illustrate, some scientists (operating on a base where Truth exists and Truth is knowable) have calculated the probability that one small protein strand in a DNA molecule could form by random chance processes. Each protein strand, they point out, is made up of a sequence of amino acids. In human DNA there are 20 different types of amino acids. These different types of amino acids attach to each other in specific sequences, and in a *small* protein strand the sequence is 150 "pieces" long. In other words, each of the 20 types of amino acids must be assembled in a precise sequence where you have 150 opportunities to get it wrong. As Chuck Missler has pointed out, if you tried to accomplish this sequence using only a process of random chance, the odds of you getting it right are 10^{195}. That number is so large it is meaningless! Let's try to unpack it a little bit. If, for the sake of argument, we grant that the universe is 12 billion years old, and you made one attempt at the correct sequence every second for 12 billion years, there are only 10^{17} seconds in the history of the universe! You're still facing insurmountable odds. Even if you made an attempt every nanosecond (every one billionth of a second), you are still facing devastating odds that are beyond improbable.

And we're talking about a small protein strand inside of a DNA molecule that is much, much more complex. And even if by a cosmic miracle you get the protein strand, or even the DNA, how are you going to explain the *information* encoded in the DNA—literally digital code?! How did the cell go from inorganic to organic matter? And our protein strand resides in a DNA molecule that resides inside of a cell that is not simple, but almost infinitely complex—like a nanotechnology factory producing software much more complicated than anything Microsoft has ever put on the market. And the cell (with the DNA and the protein strand) could be a part of the human eye, which is extraordinarily exquisite and complex in its design! And our hypothetical eye belongs to a human being who luckily lives on a planet that just happens to have the right kind of iron core, resulting in just the right kind of magnetic field around the planet (otherwise human life on earth would be impossible). And our fortunate earth also just happens to have precisely the right kind of crust (extremely thin), it has water, it has land, in fact it has the right ratio of water to land, and it has the right kind of transparent atmosphere so as to allow light to get in while maintaining just the right balance of gases, including the oxygen we breathe. The earth has a protective layer that keeps cosmic debris and radiation out, again making life possible, and it has the right kind of moon (comparatively large) which helps regulate the waters and stabilize the tilt of the earth's axis. And fortunately our hypothetical human enjoys an earth and a moon that just happen to be just the right distance from the sun to permit complex life, and the sun, luckily, just happens to be the right kind of sun, the right size of sun, and that sun emits the right kind of light, all again combining to make life possible. And the sun is part of a solar system that is located in the right kind of galaxy (ideally shaped) at a perfect location within the galaxy (most places in the galaxy are inhospitable to life). That galaxy exists in a universe which scientists say can be traced back to a singularity the size of a dime. When the singularity exploded, even Naturalistic scientists have to admit that the "explosion" was exquisitely and improbably fine-tuned—so much so that it prompted Stephen Hawking to say,

> "It would be very difficult to explain why the universe should have begun in just this way, except as an act of a God who intended to create beings like us."

Remember, if any *one* of these factors went wrong, there's no life here on earth today! And rest assured that my list is abbreviated and oversimplified! To say that all of this happened concurrently by mere chance is simply no longer tenable. (I have just made one of the all time understatements.) Could this be one of the reasons why the "scientific" estimates of the age of the universe keep expanding? Recently I was listening to a recording from ten years ago where the teacher said that the scientists were saying that the earth was six billion years old. He noted sheepishly that he was taught as a child that the earth was two billion years old. First two, then six, now they are saying 12 billion years old. You could make it 112 billion years and there still is simply not enough time to make random chance a plausible explanation for complex human life in a complex universe. It's not a credible position to take and more and more intellectually honest scientists are conceding this fact.

The moral (Natural Law), first-cause (Cosmological), and design (Teleological) arguments lead to the overwhelming conclusion that our universe has a Creator. As we have seen, this Creator has a mind that is similar to the human mind, at least in the sense of being sentient, conscious, and purposeful. The Christian Trinity gives an answer to the unity and diversity that we experience and observe in the universe. And finally we have seen that everything in the universe is *not* now as it *ought to be.*

So let's expand *The Omega Manifesto*:

4) Natural Law exists (intrinsic human morality).
5) A Lawgiver exists behind Natural Law (the Triune first cause).
6) The incredible design of the universe points to the Designer.
7) Everything in the universe is not presently as it ought to be.

Recommended Resources

Orthodoxy, G. K. Chesterton
Mere Christianity, C. S. Lewis
How Should We Then Live?, Francis Schaeffer
Trilogy, Francis Schaeffer

Steel on Steel Radio Broadcasts, www.steelonsteel.com
www.rzim.org (Ravi Zacharias)
Privileged Planet, DVD.

Chapter 3—In the Beginning . . .

As we've seen, putting on the white lab coat of science doesn't magically impart some sense of infallible objectivity to the supposedly neutral scientist. The idea is ridiculous if you think about it, yet that is what our culture would have us believe. Everybody, whether he is a scientist or not, approaches life with a set of presuppositions. The way a person sees the world is filtered through the grid of his presuppositions about the world. In the name of intellectual honesty most (hopefully) seek to be as objective as possible, but at some point an element of faith enters the equation in terms of our individual worldview. As finite creatures, we certainly cannot know everything.

C. S. Lewis rightly observed that real science does not deal with the question of whether or not there is a "something" behind the universe. Ken Ham of Answers in Genesis summarizes concisely:

> "Evolution, however, is not a scientific theory; it is a belief system about the past. . . . We cannot test the past using the scientific method (which involves repeating things and watching them happen), since all evidence we have is in the present. Evolution is a belief about the past which describes the way some people think the evidence came to be here in its present state."

The origins question is a philosophical question that begins from a position of faith—faith in evolution, or faith in a Creator. The truthfulness of the truth seeker is something which must be taken into consideration. Or, as Ravi Zacharias often says, intent is prior to content. I again defer to Ken Ham:

> ". . . The evolutionary view, as a belief system [said] there was no God, at any rate not the God of the Bible. People were and are the result of chance, i.e. no one owns you—you own yourself. This means that you are under obligation to no one. As this view became established in society, people started to ask questions such as—'If evolution is true, and there is no God who is Creator, why are there laws about marriage? Why are there laws against deviant sexual behaviour? Why are there laws at all? Why can't we take off our clothes if we want to? Why can't we carry out abortions—after all, killing a baby by abortion is like getting rid of any animal that is not needed or wanted, isn't it?' In other words, **the belief system of evolution provided a basis for the humanistic morality which said that you could do what you wanted to because nobody owned you—there was and is no right or wrong.**"

This is an important insight. What if people aren't generally atheists for intellectual reasons (due to a lack of evidence of God's existence)? What if people are generally atheists for *moral* reasons? What if atheists can't stand to live in a world that was created by a good God to whom they are morally responsible? What if, for this reason, they filter all information through a materialistic, humanistic grid? What if they *religiously* hold to the presupposition that God *can't* exist because they don't *want* Him to exist? What if George MacDonald was right when he said that to give truth to him who loves it not is to give him more multiplied reason for misinterpretation?

While there were no scientists (or creationists) around to observe the birth of our universe, isn't it interesting that the Bible claims to be inspired revelation given to humanity by the God who *was* there and *does* know what happened? Surely we would be wise to at least consider a document that claims to be an eye witness account.

6,000 Years?

So, *In the beginning*, when was that? Was it 6,000 years ago, as many conservative evangelicals claim, or was it 12 billion years ago, as many 21st century Materialistic cosmologists claim? While I'm not a mathematician, I know enough about numbers to know that you can't reconcile six thousand with 12 billion. By my math, six thousand is 1/ 2,000,000th of 12 billion. Put another way, if 6,000 years were one second, 12 billion years would be 23 days, 3 hours and change. How many readers know that there is a big difference between one second and three weeks?

The conservative evangelical starts with a Biblical worldview, examines the data, and arrives at the conclusion that the earth is 6,000 years old. The 21st century cosmologist starts with a materialistic worldview, examines the data, and arrives at the conclusion that the earth is 12 billion years old. But notice the starting point. Nobody was there to see the first moments of the universe. "The beginning" is not subject to direct observation, thus the data are not testable nor are they repeatable. The starting point is a worldview.

So, you maybe wondering, where do people get the idea that the earth is only 6,000 years old? Well, within a year of becoming a Christian I went through Genesis, Chronicles, Matthew, Luke, and other key Old and New Testament passages in order to construct my own chronology. Nobody told me to do it or even how to do it, I was just curious. Over the years I picked up two or three insights which I have here included. This is what I came up with:

Genesis 5 gives us the genealogy from Adam to Noah (10 generations):

Adam to Seth	130 years
+Seth to Enosh	105 years
+Enosh to Kenan	90 years
+Kenan to Mahalalel	70 years
+Mahalalel to Jared	65 years
+Jared to Enoch	162 years
+Enoch to Methuselah	65 years
+Methuselah to Lamech	187 years
+Lamech to Noah	182 years
=	1,056 years (#1 Adam to Noah)

From Genesis 7:6 and Genesis 11:10 it can be deduced that Noah was 502 when his son Shem was born. Noah was 600 years old in the year of the flood. Two years after the flood, Shem was 100 years old. Thus Shem was 98 years old in the year of the flood (600—98 = 502).

1056 (#1 Adam to Noah) + 502
= 1558 years (#2 Adam to Shem)

Genesis 11:10-27 gives us the genealogy from Shem to Abraham (10 generations):

Shem to Arphaxad	100 years
+Arphaxad to Shelah	35 years
+Shelah to Eber	30 years
+Eber to Peleg	34 years
+Peleg to Reu	30 years
+Reu to Serug	32 years
+Serug to Nahor	30 years
+Nahor to Terah	29 years
=	320 years (Shem to Terah)

Now, from Genesis 11:32 we know that Terah died at age 205 years old. From Acts 7:4, we know that Abraham moved to Canaan after Terah's death. Finally, we know from Genesis 12:4 that Abraham was 75 when he departed Haran for Canaan. Thus Terah was 130 years old when Abraham was born (205—75). (This also implies that Abraham was not the first born.)

Shem to Terah	320 years
+Terah to Abraham	130 years
=	450 years (Shem to Abraham)

1558 (#2 Adam to Shem) + 450
= 2008 years (#3 Adam to Abraham)

As we've already seen, Genesis 12:4 says Abraham was 75 years old when he left Harran for Canaan. Using this as the approximate time that he received the Abrahamic Covenant (Acts 7:2-3 may imply that it was given a few years earlier), we know from Galatians 3:17 that the Law was given to Moses 430 years after the Covenant was given to Abraham.

2008 (#3 Adam to Abraham) + 75 + 430
= 2513 years (#4 Adam to Mosaic Covenant).

1 Kings 6:1 says that Solomon began building his temple 480 years after Israel came out of Egypt. (Israel came out of Egypt 50 days before Moses received the Law on Mount Sinai, but for our purposes 50 days is negligible.)

2513 (#4 Adam to Mosaic Covenant) + 480
= 2993 years (#5 Adam to Solomon's Temple).

Now we have arrived at a time when the historical record is not disputed. Sure we may haggle over a few years here and there, or even a decade or two. But for our purposes here, the historical chronology from here on is essentially agreed upon by secular and theological sources alike. I will use the date 966 B.C. (somewhat arbitrarily) as the date when Solomon began to build the Temple. We live in the year 2012 A.D. Setting aside for the moment the fact that our calendar probably misses the birth of Christ by between two and five years, we arrive at the following conclusion:

  2993 (#5 Adam to building of Solomon's Temple)
+   996 (year B.C. when the Temple was constructed)
+ 2012 (current year A.D.)
———————————
= 6,001 years

Please do not view this chronology as authoritative. It should be obvious that I am not trying to construct a scholarly, watertight chronology. My guess is that this chronology is accurate to within +/- 40 years. I have not waded into the technicalities and the nuances of the issues that arise when dealing with Biblical chronologies and genealogies. Some Biblical scholars argue for gaps in the genealogical records, meaning that for every generation we see written down there could be two or three or even several generations that are *not* recorded. For this reason you'll hear many scholarly types saying that the earth is probably "less than 10,000 years old."

Many Christians, in attempting to harmonize the Bible with Humanistic science, have proposed middle-ground positions such as or Theistic evolution. Day Age theory says that each "day" of the six day creation corresponds to an epoch of the past or even to a geological age. Theistic evolution claims that God created the universe, set the evolutionary process in motion, and basically checked out. (This is a backdoor form of Deism.)

The age of the earth is a hot button issue among Christians precisely because it gets at *the way* people interpret Scripture.[3] Those who argue for a young earth approach Scripture in a more literal way. Of course there are figures of speech in the Bible and these must be taken into consideration based upon the overall context. But as a general rule those who hold to a high view of the inspiration of Scripture take what the text says at face value. Those who don't believe in the inerrancy of Scripture, on the other hand, often spiritualize the meaning of a text in a way that detracts from the literal, face-value meaning of a given passage. If one takes the entire Bible at face value, it describes a history that is at most 10,000 years in duration.

---

[3]Hermeneutics refers to the way we interpret Scripture. Hermeneutics wasn't even offered as a course at the Seminary I attended, but I took on my own through The Koinonia Institute.

Old Light, Young Universe

Now I can hear the question being asked by readers, hasn't science "proved" that the universe is billions of years old? There are many books and even entire ministries that deal competently with this question, but I do want to offer one piece of evidence (among many) which I find quite compelling. (Much of what follows I learned from Chuck Missler.)

Let's take a look at the riddle of ancient light in a young universe. One summer night when I was still a boy, I remember my grandfather taking me outside by the lake, where he said to me,

> "See that star, Sport? That star is billions of light-years away. That star might not be there anymore, but we can still see its light."

He also told me that the universe was infinite, which is what science had taught him. But we now know that the universe is bound, or finite. But returning to the question of ancient light—how can light from so far away be visible here on earth if the earth is only 6,000 years old? This seems like a formidable question indeed, but I would assert that there are reasonable explanations:

> *Measuring anything beyond 330 light years away is an inexact science and the measurements, for reasons I don't pretend to understand, are not as reliable as one might think.

> *Though a controversial subject, the speed of light appears to be slowing down. (This implies the speed of

light—C—is not a constant.) If you follow the rate at which the speed of light is slowing down backwards through history—the speed of light increasing as you go backwards in time—by the time you get to about 6,000 years ago some scientists say that the speed of light was essentially instantaneous (point to point)! Is there a theological picture being painted here?

*Time itself is a physical property that varies with mass and acceleration (Einstein's theory of relativity). Some scientists have actually calculated the gravitational potential at the hypothetical edge of the universe and, long story short, what would appear to be 12 billion years to us would appear to be six days there! How provocative is that, in light of 2 Peter 3:8—*with the Lord one day is like a thousand years, and a thousand years like one day.* 6,000 years here. Six days there!

*I don't subscribe to the notion of the uniformity of natural causes in a closed system. Basically, that all continues now as it always has. I believe in the uniformity of natural causes, yes, but not that the system is closed. God is free to intervene whenever he pleases. Obviously if people were living to 900 years and more in the time of Adam, something was drastically different about the earth and the universe. Why do we assume that the properties of light didn't change with the fall and even with the flood? Notice 2 Peter 3:3-4, *Know this first of all, that in the last days mockers will come with their mocking, following after their own lusts, and saying, "Where is the promise of His coming? For ever since the **fathers** fell asleep, **all*** *continues just as it was from the beginning of creation.*" The fathers in view in this passage are Adam and Noah and the implication is that the assumption (that all continues the same from the beginning) is false!

*Maybe the star in question really is billions of light years away, but God created the light between here and the star so we can enjoy it! Psalm 104:2 says that the Lord stretches out the heavens like a tent, maybe the Lord did just that, stretching out the universe like a slinky, the light included!

Materialistic cosmology is a moving target. The modern chronology of the universe keeps expanding, and the theories and cosmologies continue to "evolve." Besides, light is one of the least understood entities in the universe, and only recently did scientists figure out that the universe is finite. Isn't it a little silly, even arrogant, to mock the Christian position which has at least been consistent the whole time and builds its view upon a document, the Bible, which purports to be an eye witness account revealed by the God who was there and did the creating?

Gap Theory

Gap Theory is another hot button issue and just bringing it up tends to get people upset. For this reason, many pastors and Bible teachers avoid the subject altogether. Having seen the way people can act when it comes to controversies like these, I can certainly understand why. Avoidance, however, is not a tactic that I employ—at least when it comes to my pen. I will present and share my opinion on the subject, and my opinion is just that—an opinion. In the grand scheme of things we are dealing with peripheral speculation that is not worth mean-spirited fighting or even dividing over. There are good conservative evangelical scholars on both sides of the issue and I don't believe ether side should take a dogmatic position. I am including this material in *The Omega Manifesto* because it may be related to material we will get into later in the book. I also want to critique a certain segment of Evangelicalism as exemplified by their attitude concerning Gap Theory.

So (sigh), having said all of that, Gap Theory is an interesting interpretation of Genesis 1:2:

The earth was formless and void, and darkness was over the surface of the deep, and the Spirit of God was moving over the surface of the waters.

Many scholars see this verse as a seamless transition between verse one and verse three, the latter describing the first day of creation. Others aren't so sure. The debate and controversy center largely around technicalities of Hebrew grammar deriving from a conjunction and a verb. The King James Version reads:

And the earth ***was*** without form, and void.

Some hold to the view that the verse reads exactly like it should. Others claim that the phrase could, or perhaps should be rendered, ***But*** the earth ***became*** a desolate waste. Based partly on the latter translation, it is argued that there is an indefinite gap of time between Genesis 1:1 and 1:3 that allows for untold millions or even billions of years to have occurred. The alleged gap in time is often connected to Satan's rebellion and even to a pre-Adamic race that formerly inhabited the earth. (Note: Satan is already fallen when he makes his first appearance in Scripture).

Those who argue against the Gap Theory, as it is called, accuse those who argue for it of accommodating the Scriptures to modern Scientific findings. This point is well-taken. If the position is held not on the basis of Biblical evidence but on the basis of accommodating to the world spirit, then the position is self-defeating and the person who holds the view is guilty of intellectual laziness. Furthermore, those who insert millions of years and geological ages as an attempt to harmonize the earth's history with the fossil record are committing theological heresy (that's not too strong of a word). To have a fossil you need death, and the Bible teaches that by one man, Adam, death came into the world (Romans 5:12f). Gap or no gap, there is no getting around this. The origin of death is no peripheral issue either. God created a *perfect* world, Adam sinned, humanity and the world fell, and death entered the picture. This is why mankind needs a savior and this is why Jesus shed His blood. To say that God created a world where death was the norm is to undermine the very foundation of the Gospel. This is a line in the sand that must be drawn and in that respect I completely agree with those who argue against the Gap Theory.

However, grammatical issues aside (I am ignorant concerning these matters and therefore don't have a strong opinion either way), in my studies I have concluded that the Gap Theory cannot be so easily dismissed.

Something that has always intrigued me, independent of Gap Theory, is this: In Revelation 21 we read that there will be no sea and no night in the New Heaven and the New Earth (Revelation 21:1; 21:25). So my question is, why, in God's perfect creation *before* the fall, are there seas and why is there night? Symbolically in Scripture the sea and night are connected to sin and evil. On a simple level, the answer seems to be that the Lord knew the fall was coming and He was establishing a pattern. (The Lord was already teaching us before the fall occurred!) This is no shock as omniscience knows everything. Maybe I am being too mystical, but the inclusion of the sea and night in the perfect creation of Genesis 1:3 and following leaves me with the distinct impression that there could be something going on in the background that has not been explicitly stated.

At this point you could say that I am reading too much into it. But then you come to Isaiah 45:18 which reads,

> *For thus says the LORD, who created the heavens (He is the God who formed the earth and made it, He established it and did not create it a **waste place**, but formed it to be inhabited), "I am the LORD, and there is none else."*

Notice it says, *God who created the heavens*, drawing one's mind back to Genesis 1:1. Then the prophet of God parenthetically inserts, *He is the God who formed the earth and made it, He established it and did not create it a **waste place**, but formed it to be inhabited*. I checked the Hebrew, and this word translated as *waste place* is the same word which is rendered formless/without form in Genesis 1:2.

It could be that the earth was desolate in Genesis 1:2 because the Lord simlpy wasn't yet finished—that the formless earth (of verse two) refers simply to raw material that would subsequently be formed into being throughout the six days of creation. I understand this position. But there are those who believe that the state of desolation described in Genesis 1:2 came about as the result of Satan's rebellion, which included one third of the angels in Heaven (Revelation 12:4) and possibly even a pre-Adamic race. So, in my opinion, there's enough data to postulate a theory, but there's not enough to be dogmatic.

It is beyond the scope of this book to hash out the specific arguments in minute detail. As I already stated, this issue will be pertinent later on in the book, but I also bring it up now to illustrate a point that I want to make. I believe it is quite possible to hold to Gap Theory without compromising the doctrines of sin and death. Opponents of Gap Theory rarely seem to grasp this.

I strongly endorse a Didactic approach to Truth (antithesis), but I have noticed that many Christians have a tendency to draw figurative circles around themselves, the circle corresponding to their individual worldview. The Christian will then build a wall on top of that circle, which serves as a natural barrier while creating a safety zone or comfort zone. Once the wall is completed, the Christian in question often blindly refuses to accept any data from outside the wall. They then proceed to use the Didactic as a blunt weapon to eliminate anything that doesn't fall exactly in line with what they think they already know. They spell truth with a capital T, they spew endless platitudes and clichés, and they sneer that you just don't understand Scripture like they do. (I'm sorry to write so harshly but it is true.) They give simplistic answers to complex problems while labeling those who disagree with them as spiritually inferior. These people are intellectual terrorists and they are almost impossible to deal with. Mention Gap Theory on an internet message board and the Didactic trolls will come running. When you teach the Didactic approach to Truth, you will inevitably create some monsters who misapply what you are saying while labeling anything and everything they don't like as the Hegelian Dialectic.

As I understand Gap Theory, and there are others who stand with me, it isn't a way to smuggle the geological ages into the Biblical narrative. There is also no reason why Gap Theory must inherently alter the Scriptural fact that human sin and death entered through the sin of Adam. The creation that Adam enjoyed (whether it was a new creation or a recreation) was perfect. Sure there are those who use Gap Theory as a way to harmonize the Bible with an old universe and evolution. Those who do so are wrong. Yet even a great ministry like Answers in Genesis[4] (whom I am not attacking) fails to make a distinction—needlessly lumping together into the same category all who believe in Gap Theory. This baffles me. If there is a distinction that can be made, why not make it? I will not speculate as to motives I do not know, but it just seems to me to be a case of drawing circles around one's self—of the Didactic gone wrong.

In this spirit, there are a few individuals whom I respect greatly who teach that the earth is significantly older than 10,000 years, including John Ankerberg and David Flynn. While I'm not 100 percent sure that I agree with their conclusions, neither individual has compromised any of the essential

---

[4]I am NOT calling Answers in Genesis intellectual terrorists. I respect their work a great deal and have even quoted Ken Ham in this book. I am merely offering a critique.

doctrines of Christianity. In this way I am open to their ideas. I know I will endure wrath for saying that because as soon as you say anything other than 6,000 to 10,000 years, the fangs come out. At some point we have to think big picture. And right now I am merely saying that I am open to the suggestion that there *could* be more to the story than the 10,000 year paradigm to which Scripture directly speaks.

Before you write me a nasty email, please understand that I *still* believe that the *perfect* earth of Genesis 1:3 was created between six and ten thousand years ago. The question in my mind is whether or not that creation was a recreation.

So, the bottom line—who cares? What have we learned? Let's update *The Omega Manifesto:*

8) The Bible indicates that the earth, in its present form, is 6,000 to 10,000 years old.

9) The creation Adam and Eve enjoyed was originally perfect.

10) Sin and death entered through Adam, not through evolution that took place over the course of untold geological ages.

11) Gap Theory, so long as it does not contradict items 9 and 10, is an acceptable position to take.

12) A Didactic approach to Truth does not ensure that one actually possesses Truth. Didactic bullies and Truth trolls serve as small-minded examples of this fact.

Chapter 4—Bible Prophecy

The first three chapters labored to lay an essential foundation for the way we are to see the world. They also pointed out the fact that Western culture, in a monolithic way, rails against the foundation that we have established thus far. Not only does the culture assert a reality that is radically different (i.e. relative, evolving, personal, fragmented truth, materialistic Humanism, etc.), the culture attacks the worldview being asserted in *The Omega Manifesto* at a foundational level. The powers that be in our culture, from educators and the media to politicians and the entertainment industry, are not about to allow people to go on believing in Absolute Truth and Biblical Christianity. These cultural institutions have aggressively waged a war to marginalize and silence people who do believe in this way. As Francis Schaeffer points out in *The Great Evangelical Disaster*, Christianity, for the most part, has sadly rolled over and allowed it to happen. Or as John Loeffler says, we yawned and watched the parade go by! This publication, then, writes in anticipation of the coming collapse and judgment of our culture. Not that a turn-around cannot happen, for with God all things are possible. The people could certainly repent on a mass scale and throw the rascals out who are wrecking our society. But a demoralization campaign (in the Soviet sense of that term) has been successfully executed and the masses are asleep! The demise of our culture appears imminent.

In a way, every individual is responsible for allowing our nation and our culture to be hijacked by a bunch of power-tripping control freak elitists. We have been consumed by decadence and trivial vanities. Where we haven't been ignorant, we have been apathetic.

On the other hand we must certainly admit that there has been an organized campaign of evil waged against us all and that the people have been victimized. This is not a conspiracy theory in the strictest sense of that term. The cultural elitists about whom I speak have openly written about their plans for decades, arrogantly assuming that the average person would not take the time to read what they have written. Actually, they have largely been right! The average individual is not informed as to what has happened. It is this author's assertion that most people will be totally blown away by what is coming down the pike—and this will happen sooner rather than later.

Happily, Bible prophecy provides us with a strategic end-run around philosophical, political, and cultural ignorance by giving us a glimpse into where all of this is going. Let us begin with perhaps the most strategic prophecy of all.

Daniel's 70 Weeks Prophecy

This great passage in Daniel has rightly been called the spine of Bible prophecy (along with Matthew 24). Daniel 9:24-27 serves as a prophetic outline for Biblical events spanning the entire period from the 5th century B.C. to the second advent of Christ. So let's get right into the text. First, let's read the whole passage and take it all in. Then we'll go back and fill in the details.

> *"Seventy weeks have been decreed for your people and your holy city, to finish the transgression, to*

make an end of sin, to make atonement for iniquity, to bring in everlasting righteousness, to seal up vision and prophecy and to anoint the most holy place. So you are to know and discern that from the issuing of a decree to restore and rebuild Jerusalem until Messiah the Prince there will be seven weeks and sixty-two weeks; it will be built again, with plaza and moat, even in times of distress. Then after the sixty-two weeks the Messiah will be cut off and have nothing, and the people of the prince who is to come will destroy the city and the sanctuary. And its end will come with a flood; even to the end there will be war; desolations are determined. And he will make a firm covenant with the many for one week, but in the middle of the week he will put a stop to sacrifice and grain offering; and on the wing of abominations will come one who makes desolate, even until a complete destruction, one that is decreed, is poured out on the one who makes desolate."

Seventy weeks. . . . Literally seventy sevens, refers to 70 weeks of years, or 70 periods consisting of seven years.

70 x 7 = 490 years.

. . . *Have been decreed for your people and your holy city.* . . . The holy people are the Jewish people (the Church didn't exist yet) and the holy city is Jerusalem.

. . . *To finish the transgression, to make an end of sin, to make atonement for iniquity, to bring in everlasting righteousness, to seal up vision and prophecy and to anoint the most holy place.* . . . This is the purpose of the prophecy. As we will see, some of these items listed were fulfilled in the first coming of Christ, some of them will not be fulfilled until the second coming of Christ. In a broad sense some items are fulfilled in both advents.

So you are to know and discern that from the issuing of a decree to restore and rebuild Jerusalem. . . . Scholars debate precisely which Old Testament decree is in view here. The usual candidates are the decrees of Cyrus (Ezra 1:1-4), Darius I (Ezra 6:1, 6-12), or one of the two decrees pronounced by Artaxerxes (Ezra 7:11-26 and Nehemiah 2:1-8). For reasons I won't get into, the Artaxerxes decree in Nehemiah seems best, but regardless, the historical background is as follows. In 586 B.C., as a result of the judgment of God, all of Judah (Israel) had been taken away into captivity by Nebuchadnezzar and the Babylonians. Subsequently the Persians came in and took over Babylon. Thus the Jews became Persian subjects as their period of captivity continued. Then in approximately 444 B.C., King Artaxerses allowed Nehemiah to return to Judah to rebuild the city walls of Jerusalem.

. . . Until Messiah the Prince there will be seven weeks and sixty-two weeks. . . . This is saying that from the decree of King Artaxerses until the arrival of the Messiah (the seed of the woman in Genesis 3:15), there will be seven seven-year periods and 62 seven-year periods.

$$7 \times 7 = \quad 49 \text{ years}$$
$$7 \times 62 = \quad 434 \text{ years}$$
$$49 + 434 = \quad 483 \text{ years}$$

This vital passage means that from the decree (probably of Artaxerxes) until the arrival of the Messiah there would be

483 years. When you consider the fact that in 444 B.C. a different calendar system was used and also that Christ was probably born between 2 and 5 B.C., the numbers line up extremely well.

The first seven weeks (49 years) correspond to the time it took for Jerusalem to be rebuilt under Nehemiah.

. . . It will be built again, with plaza and moat, even in times of distress. . . . Jerusalem will be rebuilt. These events are described in detail in the Books of Ezra and Nehemiah.

Then after the sixty-two weeks the Messiah will be cut off and have nothing. . . .

From the completion of and rededication of Jerusalem (Nehemiah 12-13) to the "cutting off" of Messiah would be another 62 weeks (434 years). Daniel is saying that the Jews will reject the Messiah and that he will be killed. This passage was fulfilled in Luke 19 on the original Palm Sunday. In this familiar scene Jesus rides from the Mount of Olives into Jerusalem on the back of a donkey, as prophesied in Zechariah 9:9. In so doing, Jesus is declaring Himself to be King and Messiah of Israel. Luke records:

When [Jesus] approached Jerusalem, He saw the city, and wept over it, saying, "If you had known in this day, even you, the things which make for peace! But now they have been hidden from your eyes. For the days will come upon you when your enemies will throw up a barricade against you, and surround you and hem you in on every side, and they will level you to the ground and your children within you, and they will not leave in you one stone upon another, because you did not recognize the time of your visitation."

Jesus is saying that the Jews should have known the Scriptures (including Daniel 9:24-27) and recognized that it was the general season of the Messiah's first advent or appearance on earth. I would insert parenthetically here that there are those who, as soon as you mention anything about Bible prophecy and the Second Coming, make a beeline straight to *nobody knows the day or the hour* in Matthew 24:36. Yet here in Luke Jesus holds the generation of His day on earth accountable for not understanding and recognizing that, according to Scripture, it was the general time and season for the first advent to occur! Those who say that eschatology (the study of the last things) is a waste of time should take note of this. We don't know the day or hour and there have always been date-setters who make us all look bad, but that doesn't mean we can't have insight into the general time and season of the Second Coming (Matthew 16:3).

As a result of their failure to recognize the signs of the times and that He was the Messiah of Israel, Jesus said *now it is hidden from your eyes*, that is, His identity as the Messiah was hidden from their Jewish eyes. Romans 11:8 (quoting Isaiah) speaks of this same blindness:

GOD GAVE THEM A SPIRIT OF STUPOR, EYES TO SEE NOT AND EARS TO HEAR NOT, DOWN TO THIS VERY DAY.

So does 2 Corinthians 3:14-15:

But their [Jewish] minds were hardened; for until this very day at the reading of the old covenant the same veil remains unlifted, because it is removed in Christ. But to this day whenever Moses is read, a veil lies over their heart. . . .

And yet again in Romans 11:25:

For I do not want you, brethren, to be uninformed of this mystery—so that you will not be wise in your own estimation—that a partial hardening has happened to Israel until the fullness of the Gentiles has come in.

Here in Romans 11 Paul links the hardening of corporate Israel with the inclusion of the Gentiles in the Covenant blessing of Abraham. Keep that phrase in mind, *until the fullness of the Gentiles has come in.*

. . . *And the people of the prince who is to come will destroy the city and the sanctuary. And its end will come with a flood; even to the end there will be war; desolations are determined. . . .* This corresponds to what Jesus said in Luke 19:

The days will come upon you when your enemies will build an embankment against you and encircle you and hem you in on every side. They will dash you to the ground, you and the children within your walls. They will not leave one stone on another. (See also Deuteronomy 28:15ff)

Both Daniel and Luke (via Jesus) are referring to the same thing. Historically, in 70 A.D. Titus and the Roman legions laid siege to Jerusalem and completely destroyed it, including the holy temple. Just as Israel had already been taken from their own land in 586 B.C., they were removed and scattered abroad a second time in 70 A.D. This second diaspora (as it is called) scattered the Jewish people literally to the four corners of the globe.

And he will make a firm covenant with the many for one week. . . .

The prophet Daniel, as moved along by the Holy Spirit, suddenly skips ahead to the final week (seven years) of the 70 weeks prophecy (490 years), which will be fulfilled at the time of the end (the last days/the end of the age). Remember that I told you to keep in mind the phrase *until the fullness of the Gentiles has come in*? This current period, which began with the Church Age in Acts 2, in which the Gentiles are coming to salvation through faith in the Jewish Messiah Jesus of Nazareth, corresponds with the gap between the 69th and 70th week in Daniel's prophecy. Importantly, this is not the only place in Scripture where a prophet of God makes an unannounced "jump" through time. For example, look at Isaiah 61:1-2:

> *The Spirit of the Lord GOD is upon me,*
> *Because the LORD has anointed me*
> *To bring good news to the afflicted;*
> *He has sent me to bind up the brokenhearted,*
> *To proclaim liberty to captives*
> *And freedom to prisoners;*
> *To proclaim the favorable year of the LORD*
> *And the day of vengeance of our God. . . .*

Jesus quotes this Isaiah passage in Luke 4:18-19, but stops short of reading *and the day of vengeance of our God.* Why? Because the time for *the day of vengeance of our God* had not yet come (and still hasn't). Note: this is *Jesus* interpreting Scripture, and I think He knows how.

Back to the phrase *and he will make a firm covenant with the many for one week.* The personal pronoun he refers to the Biblical antichrist (the little horn of Daniel 7 and 8). 1 John 2:18 uses a definite article in connection with the antichrist, meaning that he must be an actual person. In the last days the antichrist (the false messiah of the New World Order) will make a covenant with many for one week, or seven years. As we will see, this must be a future event that has not yet occurred.

. . . *But in the middle of the week he will put a stop to sacrifice and grain offering.* . . . To the Jewish mind, this would imply that another temple will be rebuilt in Jerusalem (recall that the temple was destroyed in 70 A.D.). Put simply, Jews know that you can't have sacrifice and offering without a temple. The Dome of the Rock, that iconic golden dome that sets off the Jerusalem skyline, is built on a portion of the Temple Mount in Jerusalem—the location of the Jewish temples of old, including the one that was destroyed in 70 A.D. Thus Daniel's 70 Weeks Prophecy implies the future building of another temple in Jerusalem because to put an end to sacrifice and offering there must be sacrifice and offering taking place to begin with. The next section of the prophecy also points ahead to a yet-future fulfillment.

. . . *And on the wing of abominations will come one who makes desolate, even until a complete destruction, one that is decreed, is poured out on the one who makes desolate.* . . . Many point to Daniel chapter 11 and 12 and argue that the Abomination of Desolation is a past event, already fulfilled in history. In a sense this is true. Antiochus IV Epiphanes, in the second century B.C., went into the Jewish temple and into the Holy of Holies (the most sacred place within the temple), and slaughtered a pig on the altar—an unclean animal according to the Jewish Law. This was indeed a horrific and abominable act. But it is important to know that sometimes in Scripture past events establish patterns that point to future events. This is not sophistry but a Biblical reality. Jesus, who was certainly aware of what Antiochus IV Epiphanes had done two centuries earlier, told His disciples:

> *When you see the abomination of desolation which was spoken through the prophet Daniel . . . flee to the mountains* (Matthew 24:15).

The phrase *when you see* clearly points to a future event. There's no reason to flee to the mountains in response to an event that occurred 200 years in the past! And in case there is any remaining doubt, the Apostle Paul prophesied about this *future* Abomination of Desolation in 2 Thessalonians 2:3-4:

> *Let no one in any way deceive you, for it will not come unless the apostasy comes first, and the man of lawlessness is revealed (the antichrist), the son of destruction, who opposes and exalts himself above every so-called god or object of worship, so that he takes his seat in the temple of God, displaying himself as being God.*

The antichrist will break his seven-year covenant with many (including Israel) in the middle of the 70th week. Half of seven is 3.5 years (42 months or 1260 days in the Book of Revelation). Revelation 12:6 and other passages indicate that the antichrist will persecute Israel and the Jews for 3.5 years, that is, during the second half of Daniel's 70th Week. This last 3.5 years has been called the Great Tribulation or the Time of Jacob's trouble. Many Bible scholars believe that the future

Abomination of Desolation committed by the antichrist will kick off the Great Tribulation.

Interestingly, all of these events that Daniel prophesies will take place at some point in the future—the antichrist (the New World Order's false messiah), the seven year covenant with many, the new temple, and the Abomination of Desolation—all assume that Israel exists as a nation and that the Jewish people are dwelling in their own land. Yet between the period of 70 A.D. and 1947, nearly 2,000 years, there was no nation called Israel. But that all changed on May 14, 1948 when the modern state of Israel became a nation in a day as prophesied in Isaiah 66:8:

> *Who has heard such a thing? Who has seen such things?*
> *Can a land be born in one day?*
> *Can a nation be brought forth all at once?*
> *As soon as Zion travailed, she also brought forth her sons.*

Isaiah 11:11-12 is more specific:

> *Then it will happen on that day that the Lord*
> *Will again recover **the second time** with His hand*
> *The remnant of His people, who will remain,*
> *From Assyria, Egypt, Pathros, Cush, Elam, Shinar, Hamath,*
> *And from the islands of the sea.*
> *And He will lift up a standard for the nations*
> *And assemble the banished ones of Israel,*
> *And will gather the dispersed of Judah*
> ***From the four corners of the earth.***

Notice Isaiah says God will regather the Jews *the second time*. The Jews were removed from their land and went into the Babylonian captivity in 586 B.C. At the decree of Artaxerxes the Jews went back to Israel and back to Jerusalem to rebuild the city wall and the temple. Then in 70 A.D. (as we've seen) the Romans came and destroyed Jerusalem and the temple a second time. Yet Isaiah prophesies that the Jewish people would be regathered and taken back to their ancient homeland a second time—this time *from the four corners of the earth*.

The point is, the existence of the modern state of Israel is no historical fluke, it is the fulfillment of a very important prophecy concerning the end times that came to pass almost a generation ago. This is a significant marker that lets us know that we are in the general season of the Messiah's second coming.

The gap between Daniel's 69th and 70th weeks, corresponding to the present Church age, will not go on forever. The day is approaching when Israel will be saved and the fullness of the covenant blessings of Abraham will finally be realized. The Scriptures teach, however, that between now and then Israel and the rest of the world will pass through its darkest hour.

This is an important point. To the Christians who are sitting around waiting for the rapture to happen while relishing the coming judgment (like Jonah), this is not acceptable! The veracity and timing of the rapture aside, we *must* engage the culture war. The first three chapters of *The Omega Manifesto* establish a philosophical foundation for fighting the culture war. But at some point philosophy is worthless if all we do is sit around talking about it. We must resist and expose tyranny!

We must resist and expose the New World Order (see chapters six and seven)! But this resistance must be peaceful. He who shoots first loses! I will never endorse violence as a means of resistance. The battlefield is the public marketplace of ideas and our weapon is Truth and Love.

At the other end of the extreme are those in the liberty movement who, as an article of faith, profess a false-triumphalism that constantly pronounces the imminent demise of the New World Order. This is delusional. The best we can possibly hope to do is to forestall the inevitable—to buy time. But the New World Order *will* have its day. V for victory is a nice catch phrase, but it is not a reality that will ever be realized, at least in terms of earthly victory. Those who don't take Bible Prophecy seriously may wake up one morning surprised to find themselves on the wrong side of the ledger when the New World Order finally does arrive in all its force and fury.

If Jesus held the generation that saw His earthly ministry accountable for recognizing and understanding the times and seasons surrounding His first coming, does it not stand to reason that He will also hold accountable the generation that will see His second coming? Surely He will. This being the case, are there any additional insights that we can discern relating to the times and seasons surrounding the second advent of Christ—*without* falling into the trap of date setting?

There are certain Christian leaders and pastors who say we should avoid these discussions precisely because so many get just plain nutty when it comes to talking about Bible Prophecy. In *Orthodoxy*, G. K. Chesterton wrote:

> "Though St. John the Evangelist saw many strange monsters in his vision, he saw no creature so wild as one of his own commentators."

This point is well-taken. But we must not make the mistake of overreacting. It is certainly true that manipulative and arrogant individuals have flat out given the study of Bible prophecy a bad name. I readily concede this point, but the logical conclusion of avoiding discussion of Bible prophecy is that we have to ignore *significant* portions of Scripture. By doing so we are claiming to be smarter than God and smarter than the Holy Spirit, because evidently God thought it was a good idea to devote a great deal of time and attention to prophecies and events of the last days.

As to prophecies pertaining to the times and seasons surrounding the second coming, 2 Peter 3:8 proves quite interesting:

> *But do not let this one fact escape your notice, beloved, that with the Lord **one day is like a thousand years, and a thousand years like one day**.* [Psalm 90:4 is very similar].

Now, I've already argued for an earth (at least as we now know it) that is more or less 6,000 years old. What I did not mention until now, however, is that there is a school of thought that says that God has a 7,000 year plan for mankind. Specifically, some evangelical theologians believe that God's redemptive program for man consists of a prophetic week, each "day" corresponding to thousand-years. Let's take a moment to go down this rabbit hole. Genesis 2:17 says:

> *The LORD God commanded the man, saying, "From any tree of the garden you may eat freely; but from the tree of the knowledge of good and evil you shall not eat, for in **the day** that you eat from it you will surely die.*

A good, solid theological definition for death is simply separation. The very *day* that Adam and Eve ate of the fruit which was forbidden, they suffered spiritual death—that is, spiritual separation from God. Recall article 7 of *The Omega Manifesto*:

> 7) Everything in the universe is not presently as it ought to be.

This is *why* everything in the universe is not as it should be. In the fall man was separated from God. This means that man, even up to this present day, is not in right relationship with God his maker. What's more, not only did man fall, the whole of creation fell with him (Romans 8:22). Death, suffering, injustice, and even entropy all go back to the fall. The direct communion that Adam and Eve had enjoyed with God in the Garden of Eden was cut off. Adam died spiritually that very day.

All in all though, Adam lived a total of 930 years (Genesis 5:5). Adam suffered physical death—that is, the separation of the soul and spirit from the physical body—after about 1,000 years. *One day is like a thousand years, and a thousand years like one day.* Adam died a *spiritual* death on the actual day that he ate the forbidden fruit, but he died a *physical* death after a prophetic day of about 1,000 years. Interesting, right?

But there's more. Refer now to my chronology back in chapter 3. Note there are about 1,000 years between Adam and Noah, about 1,000 years between Noah and Abraham, about 1,000 years between Abraham and David, and about 1,000 years between David and Jesus. Thus there are about 4,000 years between Adam and Jesus—or four prophetic days.

In the New Testament, Jesus is called *the Lamb of God who takes away the sins of the world* (John 1:29). The clear implication is that Jesus Christ is the prophetic fulfillment of the Passover Lamb of the Mosaic Covenant. (The Law of Moses is the cornerstone of Judaism.) In Exodus 12, the Jewish people were instructed to tie the Passover lamb to the doorpost of the home on the 10th day of the month (Exodus 12:3). The family did not slaughter that lamb until the 14th day of the month (Exodus 12:6)—four days later. Prophetically then, could it be that before the foundation of the world, before the creation of space and time, God the Son (Jesus Christ) promised God the Father that He would die for the sins of the world (Ephesians 1:4). In other words, did Jesus tie Himself to "the doorpost of the earth" for four prophetic days, or 4,000 years? *One day is like a thousand years, and a thousand years like one day.*

That's pretty cool. Let's keep going! Hosea 6:2 reads:

He will revive us after two days;
He will raise us up on the third day,
That we may live before Him.

The "us" here in question is Israel. As we've seen, in 70 A.D. Titus and the Roman legions destroyed Jerusalem and the majority of the Jews living in Israel were scattered literally to the four corners of the earth. For almost 2,000 years, there was not nation in the world called Israel. Then in 1948, Israel became a nation again according to the terms of the UN mandate. God revived Israel after two prophetic days, approximately 2,000 years. But what of this phrase in Hosea, *He will raise us up on the third day*?

Exodus 20:11 says:

For in six days the LORD made the heavens and the earth, the sea and all that is in them, and rested on the seventh day.

Scripture clearly teaches that Christ will physically return to earth and set up a literal kingdom. This kingdom will last 1,000 years, as explicitly stated three times in Revelation 20:4-6. This Millennial (or thousand-year) Kingdom corresponds to the seventh prophetic day of rest. During the Millennial Kingdom the saints will rule and reign with Christ for a thousand years, the lion will lay down with the lamb, and the nations will beat their swords into plowshares. Thus when the prophet Hosea says *He will raise us up on the third day*, he is saying that during the Kingdom of Messiah Israel will finally enjoy the fullness of the covenant blessings promised to Abraham, including the literal kingdom promised to David.

Day	Calendar	Comment
Day 1	4000—3000 B.C.	Adam to Noah
Day 2	3000—2000 B.C.	Noah to Abraham
Day 3	2000—1000 B.C.	Abraham to David
Day 4	1000 B.C.—0 A.D.	Adam to Jesus is 4,000 years, the four prophetic days of the Passover lamb
Day 5	0—1000 A.D.	—
Day 6	1000—2000 A.D.	Israel revived after 2,000 years, two prophetic days
Day 7	2000—3000 A.D.	Millennial Kingdom

This teaching is particularly intriguing for us because we are living in the generation that saw Israel become a nation again, right on schedule. As you can see, if this scheme is true, we are bumping up against the seventh day already. But between now and then lies the seven difficult years of Daniel's 70th Week.

There is actually *another* way at getting at this same thing. I will leave it to the reader to search out whether what I am saying is true or not, but if you look at the dimensions of the Tabernacle in the Wilderness constructed by Moses and the Israelites, you will find another interesting nugget. The surface area of the outside wall of the Tabernacle, with its 60 columns, was 1,500 square cubits. Interestingly, from the time that the Law of Moses was instituted to the beginning of the Church age was about 1,500 years. In the same Tabernacle, the dimensions of the Most Holy Place were 20 x 10 x 10, which yields a net volume of 2,000 cubic cubits. Prophetically, the Most Holy Place certainly corresponds to the Church age (Acts 17:11). Could it be that the Church Age is scheduled to last *approximately* 2,000 years? (There are issues with the various calendars involved plus questions about when the precise starting point would have been, etc.) Lastly the dimensions of the Holy of Holies were 10 x 10 x 10, which yields a volume of 1,000 cubic cubits. Prophetically the Holy of Holies corresponds to the Millennial Kingdom, which of course we know lasts about 1,000 years!

I don't know about you, but all of this certainly gives me pause. No matter how you do the math, we certainly seem to be bumping up against a date with destiny! Then when I look out into the madness and craziness going on in the world, it certainly seems as if everything is developing on the world stage right on schedule.

So it's time once again to update *The Omega Manifesto*:

13) The present world order will not continue indefinitely. Christ is coming back again.
14) We appear to be in the general time and season of Christ's second coming.
15) Before Christ's second coming, the New World Order will present a false Messiah who will enter into a seven year covenant with many, including Israel.
16) We must resist and expose tyranny and the New World Order so long as we have life in our bodies.

We will deal with the coming New World Order, but first we need to dig a little deeper concerning Israel.

Chapter 5—Israel

It is not possible to understand Bible Prophecy, or the Bible for that matter, without a working knowledge of Covenant Israel in the Scriptures. And to understand Covenant Israel, it is necessary to go all the way back to the beginning, to the Book of Genesis. Genesis 1-2 deals with the creation of the heavens and the earth, and of mankind. Genesis 3 deals with the fall of mankind. After the fall of Adam and Eve, God promises that one of Adam's descendents would be the Messiah, the redeemer of all humanity. In Genesis 3:15 the Lord spoke to the serpent (Satan):

> *"And I will put enmity between you (the serpent) and the woman [Eve], and between your seed and her seed[the Messiah]; he [the Messiah] shall bruise you on the head, and you shall bruise him on the heel."*

Genesis chapters 4 to 11 are basically the story of the bloodline that would produce that seed (the Messiah) from Adam to Abraham. The narrative includes a global worldwide flood brought about as God's judgment on a rebellious human race. Only Noah and his immediate family were spared. In preserving Noah and his family from the judgment of the flood, the promised seed of the woman is also preserved. After the flood the earth repopulated only to organize an economic, political, and spiritual rebellion under the leadership of Nimrod. God judged this rebellion by scattering the nations and confusing the languages.

In this context Genesis 11 introduces us to Abram (the 20th generation from Adam), who was later renamed Abraham. Abraham (as I will call him) is therefore presented as the seed of Adam and Noah and it is thus implied that the Messiah promised in Genesis 3:15 will be a descendant of Abraham.

Genesis 12:1-3 teaches us exactly that:

Now the LORD said to Abram,
"Go forth from your country,
And from your relatives
And from your father's house,
To the land *which I will show you;*
*And I will make you **a great nation**,*
And I will bless you,
And make your name great;
*And so you shall be a **blessing**;*
And I will bless those who bless you,
And the one who curses you I will curse
And in you all the families of the earth will be
*   blessed."*

God promised Abraham a land—which would come to be known as geographical Israel. He also promised that his offspring would form a people to populate the land (Israelites, Hebrews, Jews, Israelis). Finally the Lord promised Abraham blessing. So God promised Abraham a land, a people, and blessing.

The LORD appeared to Abram and said, "To your descendants I will give this land" (Genesis 12:7).

This is the foundation of what theologians call the Abrahamic covenant. Notice that the initiative was all on God's side. God approached Abraham unilaterally and promised him a land, a people, and blessing without condition. God didn't say to Abraham, "If you do what is right this will be your reward." No, the Lord promised the land, the people, and the blessing unconditionally.

The problem was, Abraham and his wife Sarah were getting up there in age. To say it in a less tactful way, they were old! And they were childless. Despite the circumstances, God promises Abraham a son in Genesis 15:4:

> *Then behold, the word of the LORD came to him, saying, "This man (Ishmael) will not be your heir;* ***but one who will come forth from your own body, he shall be your heir."***

Following a faithless episode with a maidservant resulting in the birth of Ishmael, the Lord makes it clear that Ishmael would not be the heir of the covenant promise (as the Islamic religion claims). Genesis 17:18-21:

> *And Abraham said to God, "Oh that Ishmael might live before You!"*

> *But God said, "No, but Sarah your wife will bear you a son, and you shall call his name Isaac; and I will establish My covenant with him for an everlasting covenant for his descendants after him. As for Ishmael, I have heard you; behold, I will bless him, and will make him fruitful and will multiply him exceedingly. He shall become the father of twelve princes, and I will make him a great nation.* ***But My covenant I will establish with Isaac,*** *whom Sarah will bear to you at this season next year."*

The descendants of Abraham who would populate the Promised Land (Israel) and who would enjoy the covenant blessings would come through Isaac, not Ishmael.

Isaac then had two twin sons, Jacob and Esau (Genesis 25:26). The Genesis account records that Esau sold his birthright—the covenant blessing—to Jacob for a pot of stew (Genesis 25:27-34). Later Jacob, through trickery, formally received the blessing from his father Isaac (Genesis 27). Thus the blessings enjoyed by covenant Israel came down through Abraham, Isaac, and Jacob, the fathers of Israel—the Jewish people.

Jacob had twelve sons who became the fathers of the 12 respective tribes of Israel (Genesis 30). Genesis 37 introduces us to Joseph, one of the 12 sons of Jacob. The remainder of Genesis is concerned with the details of Joseph's life and the whole point, especially for our purposes, is how and why Jacob and his 12 sons went down into Egypt as a small tribe of 70 people (as prophesied in Genesis 15:13). This is how the Book of Genesis concludes. This is not just a nice story, this small tribe of 70 people are the heirs of the covenant blessing promised to Abraham in Genesis 12:1-3 (also Genesis 15, 17, 22, etc.). This is the story of the Jewish people, who would produce the promised Messiah of Genesis 3:15.

The Book of Exodus begins as follows:

But the sons of Israel were fruitful and increased greatly, and multiplied, and became exceedingly mighty, so that the land was filled with them (Exodus 1:7).

The small tribe of 70 became a full-fledged nation. The Egyptian Pharaoh was politically threatened by the growing minority group and responded by subjugating the Hebrew people (as they came to be called). Within this context, a few generations later God raised up Moses to be the deliverer of Israel. (Moses is a type of Christ.) Through signs and wonders, God brought Israel out of Egypt into the wilderness where He gave them The Ten Commandments (see Exodus 1-20).

Three Covenants

The Ten Commandments served as the foundation of the Mosaic Covenant and Judaism. But, and this is important, the Mosaic Covenant was given within the broader context of the Abrahamic Covenant. The relationship between these two covenants is a necessary but neglected study. While the Abrahamic Covenant was unconditional and eternal, the Mosaic Covenant was conditional and temporary. For example, Deuteronomy 28, referring to the Mosaic Covenant, lists specific blessings that would follow if the children of Israel were obedient and it lists specific curses and judgments should they be disobedient.

The Mosaic Law instituted ordinances, priests, and sacrifices which were to provide temporary atonement for the sins of Israel. God is the source of Absolute Truth in the universe and our concept of right and wrong derives from Him. God created a perfect universe which subsequently fell as a result of Adam's sin. As a result of the fall, all of mankind has inherited a sin nature that separates us from God and compromises our having a right relationship with Him. At its heart, the Law was not given as a moral code for humanity to follow. The point of the Law was to show its adherents (the Jews and gentile converts) their utter inability to keep the Law and the impossibility of living up to the absolutely perfect standards of an all-Holy God. In short, the Law shows humanity its need for redemption. It shows us our need for the Messiah-redeemer promised in Genesis 3:15. The Law was not designed as *a system to achieve salvation*. This is radical revelation for a Biblically illiterate generation! The following Scriptures support these audacious claims:

Hebrews 10:1-4 (NIV):

The law is only a shadow of the good things that are coming—not the realities themselves. For this reason it can never, by the same sacrifices repeated endlessly year after year, make perfect those who draw near to worship. Otherwise, would they not have stopped being offered? For the worshipers would have been cleansed once for all, and would no longer have felt guilty for their sins. But those sacrifices are an annualreminder of sins. It is impossible for the blood of bulls and goats to take away sins.

2 Corinthians 3:13:

[We] are not like Moses, who used to put a veil over his face so that the sons of Israel would not look intently at the end of what was fading away [the Law].

These two verses point to the temporary nature of the Mosaic Covenant. The Law is described as *a shadow of the good things that are coming* and as *fading away*. Keep this in mind. The next two verses identify the purpose of the Law:

. . . Because by the works of the Law no flesh will be justified in His sight; for through the Law comes the knowledge of sin (Romans 3:20).

And,

Now that no one is justified by the Law before God is evident; for, "THE RIGHTEOUS MAN SHALL LIVE BY FAITH" (Galatians 3:11).

According to Romans 7:13 the Law shows the sinfulness of sin. The Law was always intended to be a temporary and imperfect solution pointing forward to the permanent and perfect solution that would come only in the sacrificial death of Jesus Christ. The Law shows us that we are utterly incapable of keeping the Law. It serves as a mirror exposing our own sinfulness before God who is perfect.

I know this is a little tedious but please keep reading because this is very important. Let's keep digging here. Galatians 3:16-17 speaks directly to the relationship between the Abrahamic and Mosaic Covenants.

Now the promises [the Abrahamic Covenant—land, people, blessing] *were spoken to Abraham and to his seed. He (the Lord) does not say, "And to seeds," as referring to many, but rather to one, "And to your seed," that is, Christ. What I am saying is this: the Law* [the Mosaic Covenant]*, which came four hundredand thirty years later, does not invalidate the* [Abrahamic] *covenant previously ratified by God, so as to nullify the promise.*

The Law, the Mosaic Covenant, does not nullify the promise—the Abrahamic Covenant. Thus we have established the temporary and imperfect nature of the Mosaic Covenant. We have seen that the purpose of the Mosaic Covenant was to reveal our sin nature and need for a Savior. And we have seen that the Mosaic Covenant was given within the broader context of the Abrahmic Covenant and that the Mosaic Covenant does not abrogate the Abrahamic Covenant.

The Gospel

We now have a sufficient foundation for the Gospel of Jesus Christ. Where you and I can never keep the Law perfectly, Jesus Christ came and fulfilled the Law perfectly (Matthew 5:17; Romans 10:4). This was the *basis* for his sacrifice on the cross. The imperfect, finite, repetitious sacrifices of bulls and goats only pointed forward to the perfect, infinite, once-for-all sacrifice of Christ. Based upon the perfect, sinless life of Christ, the Father counted Him worthy to be the sacrificial offering on behalf of you and I. When Jesus Christ was executed and died, He bore the punishment due you and I because of our sins. This is the foundation of the Christian message of salvation. In a way, this is how the story ends. In another way, the story is anything but over . . . it's just beginning.

Appropriately, in Luke 22:20 Jesus instituted the New Covenant. The question arises then, what was the Old Covenant? Which Covenant is Jesus replacing? Does the New Covenant replace the Abrahamic or the Mosaic—the promise of the Law? (God made a covenant with David as well, the Davidic Covenant, but that's a story for another day.) The answer should already be clear from what we have studied up

to this point. While the Abrahamic Covenant was unconditional and eternal, the Mosaic Covenant was conditional and
temporary. The Law does not nullify the promise (of Abraham). Jeremiah 31:31-33 confirms this:

> Behold, days are coming," declares the LORD,
> "when I will make a new covenant with the house of
> Israel and with the house of Judah, not like the
> covenant which I made with their fathers in the day
> I took them by the hand to bring them **out of the
> land of Egypt**, My covenant which they broke,
> although I was a husband to them," declares the
> LORD. But this is the covenant which I will make
> with the house of Israel after those days," declares
> the LORD, "I will put **My law** within them and on
> their heart I will write it; and I will be their God,
> and they shall be My people."

Without a doubt, Moses is in view here, not Abraham.
The New Covenant replaces the Law. Ezekiel 36:26 says:

> Moreover, I will give you a new heart and put a new
> spirit within you; and I will remove the heart of
> stone from your flesh and give you a heart of flesh.

Through faith in Christ, God makes the believer into a
new creation (2 Corinthians 5:17; John 3:3, etc.) giving him a
new nature. God writes His Law on the believer's heart. The
transformational (not in the dialectical sense of that term)
power of the Holy Spirit enables believers to keep the Law
where they couldn't do so before. The heart of stone is a clear
reference to the stone tablets on which the Ten Command-

ments were written. The heart of flesh is a regenerated, born-again heart that has repented and believed in the Gospel of Christ. [Therefore to assert that the New Covenant is grace without law is absolutely contrary to the Scriptures. Those who love the Lord keep His commandments (John 14:15).]

What of Israel?

Now that we know that the Mosaic Covenant doesn't replace the Abrahamic Covenant and that the New Covenant replaces the Mosaic Covenant (not the Abrahamic Covenant), what is the relationship between the Abrahamic Covenant and the New Covenant? What does this mean for the future of Israel? Is the Church the spiritual fulfillment of the blessing promised to Abraham? Does the Church supplant Israel in God's plan?

The relationship between the New Covenant and the Abrahamic Covenant is the same as the relationship between the Abrahamic Covenant and the Mosaic Covenant. The New Covenant is to be viewed within the broader context of the Abrahamic Covenant. To illustrate, envision the Patriarch of monotheism, Abraham. His body represents the Abrahamic Covenant. Now picture the stone tablets of the Ten Commandments placed on Abraham's chest, where his heart would normally be. The stone tablets represent the Mosaic Covenant. Now picture the stone tablets being removed from Abraham's chest and replaced by a heart. The heart of flesh (as Ezekiel puts it) has the same Law written on it. The new heart represents the New Covenant!

Some Christians teach that the New Covenant replaces the Abrahamic Covenant. This is a misunderstanding. Recall that God unilaterally and unconditionally promised Abraham a land, a people, and blessing (Genesis 12:3). Between the birth of the Church and the present day a temporary blinding has been upon the Jewish people as a whole. The restoration of the Jews to their ancient homeland in 1948 marked the beginning of God's final restoration of the Jewish people in history. God will keep His unconditional promise. Can I back up these claims Biblically and theologically?

The answer is an emphatic yes! Paul teaches New Testament readers about Israel's future in no uncertain terms. As we saw in the previous chapter, the whole of Romans 11 deals with this issue. Many Evangelicals rightly point to Romans 11 as obvious proof that the Church has not replaced Israel in God's redemptive and prophetic program for the earth. But I believe it is important to deal with the relationship of the Covenants as well (as we have now done). In fact, I did not read my analysis of the relationship between the Covenants anywhere, I just went through the Scriptures and sorted it out on my own. Not that writings don't exist, I just have never seen them. I'm sure that Dr. Arnold Fructenbaum's *Israelogy* deals with these Covenant issues but I have not had the opportunity to read that famous work. The point is that Romans 11 is a key chapter indeed, but there is much more evidence in Scripture to support the view that I am asserting (that the Church does not replace Israel). I encourage you to read the entire 11th chapter of Romans on your own, but let's take a look at portions of it right now:

> *I say then, God has not rejected His people, has He? May it never be! For I too am an Israelite, a descendant of Abraham, of the tribe of Benjamin. God has not rejected His people whom He foreknew. . . .* (verses 1-2)

I say then, they did not stumble so as to fall, did they? May it never be! But by their transgression salvation has come to the Gentiles, to make them jealous. Now if their transgression is riches for the world and their failure is riches for the Gentiles, how much more will their fulfillment be! (verses 11-12)

This goes back to the blinding that occurred in Luke 19 and it implies the gap between the 69th and 70th weeks in Daniel's 70 Weeks Prophecy. Continuing:

And they (Israel) also, if they do not continue in their unbelief, will be grafted in, for God is able to graft them in again (verse 23).

For I do not want you, brethren, to be uninformed of this mystery—so that you will not be wise in your own estimation—that a partial hardening has happened to Israel until the fullness of the Gentiles has come in; and so all Israel will be saved (verses 25-26).

*. . . For the gifts and the calling of God (the blessings of the Abrahamic Covenant) **are irrevocable.*** (verse 29).

This is very straightforward and falls in line quite neatly with what we have learned about the Covenants. Some readers may say, well sure, Jewish people can be saved, they just need to join the Church! Of course salvation is in Jesus alone (John 14:6), but Jesus is the *Jewish Messiah*. For the most part, the Jews have rejected Him to date (although there are more Messianic Jews alive today than ever before, even in Jerusalem!). Thus the Jews have yet to enjoy the fullness of the blessing of the Abrahamic Covenant. Importantly, there is a body of Scripture in the Hebrew Old Testament that can *only* be fulfilled when the Jewish people accept their Jewish Messiah. (These prophecies have little or nothing to do with the Gentile Church which was a mystery unknown in the Old Testament era.)

I want to point out one more Scripture that is the final nail in the coffin for Replacement Theology (the view that the Church permanently replaces Israel in God's plan). That passage is Ezekiel 36:22-32:

> *"Therefore say to the house of Israel, 'Thus says the Lord GOD, "**It is not for your sake, O house of Israel, that I am about to act**, but for **My holy name**, which you have profaned among the nations where you went. I will vindicate the holiness of My great name which has been profaned among the nations, which you have profaned in their midst. Then the nations will know that I am the LORD,"** declares the Lord GOD, "when I prove Myself holy among you in their sight.*
>
> *"**For I will take you from the nations, gather you from all the lands and bring you into your own land.** Then I will sprinkle clean water on you, and you will be clean; I will cleanse you from all your filthiness and from all your idols. Moreover, I will give you a new heart and put a new spirit within you; and I will remove the heart of stone from your*

flesh and give you a heart of flesh. I will put My Spirit within you and cause you to walk in My statutes, and you will be careful to observe My ordinances. **You will live in the land that I gave to your forefathers; so you will be My people, and I will be your God.** *Moreover, I will save you from all your uncleanness; and I will call for the grain and multiply it, and I will not bring a famine on you. I will multiply the fruit of the tree and the produce of the field, so that you will not receive again the disgrace of famine among the nations. Then you will remember your evil ways and your deeds that were not good, and you will loathe yourselves in your own sight for your iniquities and your abominations.* **I am not doing this for your sake," declares the Lord GOD, "let it be known to you. Be ashamed and confounded for your ways, O house of Israel!"**

God will bring about what He promised to Abraham (a land, a people, and blessing) not because of Israel's faithfulness. No, Israel has been profoundly unfaithful during the period in which they have been scattered to the four corners of the earth. (This is why they have endured the curses of Deuteronomy 28:15 and following while they have lived among the nations following the destruction of the Temple and the capturing of Jerusalem in 70 A.D.) In the end, God keeps His promise to Abraham for the sake of His holy name. He unilaterally and unconditionally promised Abraham a land, people, and blessing, and He will deliver on His promise. Again, in 1948 God began to move on this promise. The new heart passages of Jeremiah 31 and Ezekiel 36 can rightly be applied to born-again Gentile Christians, but these passages ultimately will be fulfilled in the salvation of corporate Israel.

Replacement Theology

The following is the final paper I wrote for the Hermeneutics course I took through Chuck Missler's Koinonia Institute (based in Coeur d'Alene, Idaho). I was in Seminary at the time pursuing my Master's degree and I thought it absurd that Hermeneutics wasn't even offered at the seminary I was attending. So I took it upon myself to take the course. I mention that because the paper is on the academic side, which accounts for the extensive footnoting. I would also preface this paper by stating that my views on radical Islam are currently a bit more nuanced. The article also quotes John Hagee, an individual I wouldn't entirely endorse at present. Also, several of the articles come from the Pre-Trib Research Center. This is not necessarily a commentary on my position on that subject. Finally, a little bit of the material in the middle of the paper repeats what I have just said, but it presents the material in a different way. Some may actually find this small amount of repetition helpful. That said, here is that paper on Replacement Theology, which I believe was written in late 2006 or early 2007. (Scripture quotations are from the King James Version of the Bible.) Replacement Theology "is the view that the church is the new or true Israel that has permanently replaced or superseded Israel as the people of God."[1] This Ecclesiological position is known by varying names including Supersessionism, Covenant Theology, and Restoration Theology, and is also the prevailing view of the Kingdom Now / Dominion Theology movement. This position, that the

Church "replaces" Israel while inheriting the covenant blessings of Abraham, is widespread among main-line denominational churches in America. Though the statistics are a bit dated [even more so now], the following list may help to illustrate the predominance of Replacement Theology in the United States. The name of the Church / denomination is followed by the estimated number of U.S. adherents as of 2004:

The Roman Catholic Church—66,407,105
The United Methodist Church—8,251,042
Evangelical Lutheran Church in America—5,038,006
Presbyterian Church (U.S.A.)—3,407,329
The Lutheran Church—Missouri Synod—2,512,714
African Methodist Episcopal Church—2,500,000
The Episcopal Church—2,333,628
Churches of Christ, Corsicana, Texas—1,500,000
Greek Orthodox Archdiocese of America—1,500,000
African Methodist Episcopal Zion Church—1,430,795
United Church of Christ—1,330,985
Christian Churches and Churches of Christ,
    Joplin, Missouri—1,071,616[2]

Represented in this list are nearly 100 million Americans and 12 of the largest 23 Church bodies in the United States. (My list excludes the LDS Church and the Jehovah's Witnesses, though technically they too espouse a form of Replacement Theology.) By comparison, the list's remaining 11 Church denominations, who traditionally reject Replacement Theology, claim only 43.2 million members.[3] Grant Jeffrey was correct when he asserted that "there is a major division growing between churches and denominations over Israel's role in God's plan today."[4]

This essay will seek to demonstrate the following: 1) Replacement Theology is the theological rational behind two millennia of murderous anti-Semitism. 2) One's view of Replacement Theology will inevitably affect one's view of Ecclesiology (view of the Church) and Eschatology (view of the Last Things). 3) Fundamentally, to embrace Replacement Theology is to impugn God's character. 4) The fanatical anti-Semitism behind radical Islam is the logical conclusion of Islam's own brand of Replacement Theology.

From Augustine to Auschwitz

It may sound unreasonable at first, but Replacement Theology played a major part in paving the way towards Hitler's holocaust. The story begins all the way back during the days of the early Church. (What follows is admittedly greatly oversimplified.) According to Dr. Thomas Ice, around A.D. 160 Justin Martyr was the first to espouse the view that "the Christian church [is] 'the true spiritual Israel.' "(5) Taking the next step down the slippery slope was the hugely influential theologian and scholar Origen (185—ca. 254 A.D.). Origen began to develop a system of allegorizing the Scriptures— rejecting the literal hermeneutics of other Church Fathers.(6) Origen's allegorical approach, which lends itself to the Church replacing Israel, inspired Augustine (354-430 A.D.)— perhaps the most influential theologian in the history of the Western Church. (Augustine was a Replacement Theologian.) Add Augustine's theological backing to the powerful emerging Church-State dynamic, and the unfortunate recipe for anti-Semitic disaster was well-nigh established. (After all, the literal pre-millennial view of the Scriptures was and is inherently antithetical to a Church-State system seeking to subdue the world.)(7) The stage was set for the Crusades and the Inquisitions. Lest the reader think the case is being overstated, listen to the venomous words of Augustine's contemporary John Crysostom (349-407 A.D.), widely considered to be the most prominent preacher of his day:

"The Jews are the most worthless of all men. They are lecherous, greedy and rapacious. They are perfidious murders of Christ. They worshiped the devil; their religion is a sickness. The Jews are the odious assassins of Christ, and for killing God there is no expiation possible, no indulgence or pardon. Christians may never cease vengeance, and the Jews must live in servitude forever. God always hated the Jews. It is incumbent upon all Christians to hate the Jews."(8)

I believe that Dr. Ice is justified in making the following statement:

"Replacement theology has been the fuel that has energized Medieval anti-Semitism, Eastern European Pogroms, the Holocaust and contemporary disdain for the modern state of Israel."(9)

Dr. Chuck Missler calls it the "road from Augustine to Auschwitz."(10) Dave Hunt explains:

"Hitler justified his 'final solution' by pointing out that the [Catholic] Church had oppressed and killed Jews for centuries. How amazing that those who claimed to be the followers of Christ and successors of Peter could 'persecute the race from which Peter—and Jesus—sprang'! Yet they did it in the name of Christ and felt justified thereby."(11)

An Issue for Today

Whether they know it or not, many Evangelical and Protestant Churches in the West have inherited Augustine's view of the Church as Israel. Dr. Ice explains:

"The church often allegorizes many portions of the Bible, both Old and New Testaments, in order to teach that since the time of Christ Israel has no claim to the land of Israel."(12)

Dr. J. Randall Price writes in an article entitled *Is the Modern State of Israel Prophetically Significant?*:

"There are also Catholic, Protestant, and Reformed Churches in the West who, while accepting the political reality of the modern Jewish state, deny any theological importance to Jewish regathering."(13)

This would help to explain why it took the Vatican 46 years to recognize the existence of the modern State of Israel.(14) This would help to explain why the Presbyterian Church U.S.A. called for divestment from its holdings connected to Israeli interests.(15) This would help to explain "widespread unbalanced media reporting" of events in Israel and the Middle East.(16) This would help to explain why, indirectly, Replacement Theology is official United States foreign policy.(17) This would help to explain why, as Dr. J. Randall

Price reports, many Eastern Churches "view the existence of the State of Israel, and especially Judaism, as an intrusion into a religious situation dominated by their ecclesiastical bodies since the early centuries of Christianity. From their shared theological perspective of replacement theology, they are the rightful successors of the ancient church and therefore of the old Israel and consider themselves to be a part of the Land in their own right."[18]

Dr. Price continues:

"For this reason the modern rebirth of the Jewish state is seen as of no special importance. This theological attitude is more or less held by churches in the West, who, with churches in the East must enter into conflict with the Jewish state over political and property issues or in protests of the Israeli government's treatment of the resident Christian community, the larger percentage of which is Palestinian Arab."[19]

In an article entitled *Christian Zionism* Dr. Thomas Ice states,

"If the Bible is to be taken literally and still applies to Israel . . . it should not be surprising to anyone that such a view leads one, such as myself, to Christian Zionism. Zionism is simply the desire for the Jewish people to occupy the land of Israel. Christian Zionists are Christians who advocate this belief."[20]

Dr. Ice notes that while Christian Zionism is on the rise, so too is its opposition. It appears that the issue of Israel is increasingly a watershed issue for the Church.

God's Character Is on the Line

In his new book *Epicenter,* Joel Rosenberg chooses his side:

". . . Second, as an evangelical Christian, I believed what the Bible said about God giving the land of Israel to the Jewish people as an everlasting covenant, one that could not be broken, no matter what mistakes we Jews made throughout the centuries."[21]

Rosenberg's remarks bring us to the heart of the matter. The issue of Replacement Theology is not primarily about Ecclesiology, Eschatology, or getting back to our Jewish roots —as important as these issues are for born-again Christians. The real issue is the integrity of God's promises to Abraham and the Jewish people. Chapters 12, 15, and 17 of Genesis state plainly enough that the Abrahamic Covenants are unconditional and everlasting. And the Hebrew word used repeatedly for everlasting means, yes, everlasting! By all accounts the Mosaic Covenants were conditional or performance-based, and Paul addresses this issue head-on in Galatians 3:17-18:

And this I say, that the covenant, that was confirmed before of God in Christ, the law, which was four hundred and thirty years after, cannot disannul, that it should make the promise of none effect. For if the inheritance be of the law, it is no more of promise: but God gave it to Abraham by promise.

Ezekiel 36 in its proper context makes it very clear that ultimately God fulfills His promises to Abraham, not because of Israel's obedience, but for the sake of His Holy name. Verses 22 states emphatically:

Therefore say unto the house of Israel, thus saith the Lord GOD; I do not this for your sakes, O house of Israel, but for mine holy name's sake, which ye have profaned among the heathen, whither ye went.

When applied to a literal and future event, there can be no doubt as to what Ezekiel 36 is referring. Isaiah 11:11 makes it clear that Israel would be scattered among the nations twice. Hosea 6:2 hints that the second diaspora would last about 2000 years. Taken at face value, Daniel 9:24-27 explains that this mysterious 2,000 year interval is 'filled in' by the Church. And finally, Romans 11 explicitly states that Israel's blindness, initiated by Jesus in Luke 19, is temporary. The original Jewish branches will be grafted back in!

Galatians 6:16 is the only verse that can possibly be used to argue that the Church replaces Israel—but even that is a contrivance once the grammar is carefully analyzed, especially in light of Galatians 6:15. I know it sounds harsh, but I agree with Grant Jeffrey:

"Some Christians still reject the clear teaching of the Old and New Testaments about the role of Israel in God's plan for the redemption of the planet. The Bible declares that Israel's covenant with God is unbroken. Israel is still the key to the unfolding prophetic events leading to the second coming of Christ. Since these prophetic Scriptures are unshakable, the only way to escape their clear message is to arbitrarily *change the meaning* of the Bible's words (emphasis added)."(22)

Dr. Ice agrees, stating,

"Since Israel is a subject found on just about every page of the Old and New Testaments, to get that subject wrong can only lead to a mega-distortion of Scripture. This has indeed been the case throughout the history of the church."(23)

In an article entitled *The Kingdom of God*, Dave Hunt asserts,

"Thus to deny Israel that special part in prophecy, and to claim that the church is now Israel, removes foundational points of reference and opens the door to distortion and confusion both as to Israel and the church."(24)

In another article entitled *Jews, Gentiles & the Church*, Hunt states,

"The preservation of the Israelis as an identifiable people, in spite of the proverbial 'wandering Jews' 2,000-year Diaspora from the promised land, and the establishment of Israel in 1948, constitute irrefutable proof for the existence of the 'God of Abraham, Isaac and Jacob' and the validity of His Holy Word. Therefore, to insist that Israel no longer has any claim to her ancient homeland, and that her return thereto is a mere coincidence, denies one of the most persuasive arguments for belief in God and the gospel."(25)

In his classic book *The Late Great Planet Earth*, Hal Lindsey says succinctly,

"Some theologians of the liberal school still insist that prophecy has no literal meaning for today and that it cannot be taken seriously. It is difficult to understand this view if one carefully weighs the case of Israel's rebirth as a nation."[26]

Dr. Dwight Pentecost, long-time professor at Dallas Theological Seminary, summarizes:

"Thus we conclude that the church is a part of a kingdom of the God of heaven, falling in the inter-advent period. It was an unrevealed mystery in the Old Testament, but it was necessitated by Israel's rejection of the Messiah, which caused the post-ponement of the promised and covenant form of the kingdom, which will be inaugurated by the appear-ance of the King of kings and Lord of lords at His second advent."[27]

Recently while reading E. W. Bullinger's *The Witness of the Stars* (originally published in 1893), I encountered the following:

"If we ask how long [Jerusalem] shall continue to be 'trodden down'? how long it will be before Israel shall again possess their city and their land?—the answer brings us at once to the heart of our subject."[28]

And again, remember this was first published in 1893:

"Though Jews are returning thither in ever-increas-ing numbers, they are only strangers there. They have as yet no independent position, nor can they make any treaties. But when the 'times' shall end, it means that they will have a position of sufficient independence to be able to make a treaty or league with the coming Prince (Dan. ix. 27); and then the course of events will bring on another treading down of 1260 literal 'days,' which will thus have had a fore-shadowing fulfillment in years! This is written in Rev. xi. 2. And to save us from any mis-understanding, the time is given, not in days, but in '*months*' (emphasis added)."(29)

Not that I should have been surprised, but I was delighted by the idea that Bullinger was anticipating Isaiah 66:8 (the rebirth of Israel) 55 years before the fact!

Replacement Theology and Islam

Our discussion of Replacement Theology concludes with a brief examination of Islam. Rabbi Jeff Adler of Shaarey Yeshua Messianic Congregation (Indianapolis, IN) told me flat out, "Replacement theology is the heart of Islam."(30) After all, Muslims teach that it was Ishmael, not Isaac, who was Abraham's 'Son of Promise' offered on Mount Moriah. Thus God's blessings allegedly came down through the Arab offspring of Ishmael. Hal Lindsey notes in *The Everlasting Hatred, the Roots of Jihad* that "in their zeal to replace Israel, the Muslim's most serious charge against the Jews is that they corrupted the revelation God gave them."(31) Islam teaches that the Koran abrogates the Bible of the Jews and Christians, and that it is the full and final revelation of Allah—who is supposedly the same god as the God of the Bible. In making these claims, Islam clearly attempts to usurp God's promises and covenants with the Jews.

At its core, Islam is inherently anti-Semitic. Let the Koran speak for itself:

Sura 2:96 And you will most certainly find them [Jews] the greediest of men for life (greedier) than even those who are polytheists.

Sura 3:112 Abasement is made to cleave to them [Jews] wherever they are found, except under a covenant with Allah and a covenant with men, and they have become deserving of wrath from Allah, and humiliation is made to cleave to them; this is because they disbelieved in the communications of Allah and slew the prophets unjustly; this is because they disobeyed and exceeded the limits.

Sura 4:46 . . . But Allah has cursed them [Jews] on account of their unbelief, so they do not believe but a little.

Sura 5:51 O you who believe! do not take the Jews and the Christians for friends; they are friends of each other; and whoever amongst you takes them for a friend, then surely he is one of them; surely Allah does not guide the unjust people.

Sura 5:60 Say: Shall I inform you of (him who is) worse than this in retribution from Allah? [Worse is he (Jews)] whom Allah has cursed and brought His wrath upon, and of whom He made apes and swine, and he who served the Shaitan; these [Jews] are worse in place and more erring from the straight path.

The Islamic Hadith (traditions attributed to the Prophet Mohammad) fall in line with the Koran:

"The Resurrection of the dead will not come until the Muslims will war with the Jews and the Muslims will kill them. The trees and rocks will say, 'O Muslim, here is a Jew behind me, come and kill him.' "(32)

Unbelievably, the destruction of the Jews is a pre-requisite for the Islamic version of the Last Days. No wonder the

Palestinian Authority charter openly calls for the destruction of Israel. No wonder Saddam Hussein launched scuds at Israel in 1991. No wonder Iranian president Mahmoud Ahmadinejad is openly denying the holocaust and calling for Israel to be wiped off the face of the map. No wonder Ahmadinejad believes he is on a mission from Allah to cause a global conflagration that will hasten the emergence of the 12th Imam— the Islamic leader who will lead the Last Days charge against the Jews. No wonder Islamic radicals dream of the day when they will push the Jews into the Mediterranean Sea.

One of the most powerful films I have viewed is Honest Reporting's *Relentless*. This film documents the indoctrination of hatered of the Jews perpetrated on young children at PA funded schools. How my blood boiled when I saw a five year old holding a machine gun and telling the camera that his highest goal in life was to kill Jews. This evil is straight out of the pit of hell.

Some theologians and Biblical scholars teach that Satan believes that if he can annihilate every Jew on the face of the earth, he can show God to be a liar and therefore derail the Second Coming. Matthew 23:39 seems to support this idea. Jesus Himself says that He will not return until the Jews say, *Blessed is He who comes in the name of the Lord*. Obviously if there are no Jews to cry out, then Jesus cannot return. (At least that's the idea.)

According to the estimates, Hitler succeeded in killing at least 6 million European Jews, roughly one-third of the worldwide Jewish population at the time. Zechariah 13:8 indicates that the coming antichrist will succeed in killing *two*-thirds of the Jews living in his day:

And it shall come to pass, that in all the land, saith the LORD, two parts therein shall be cut off and die; but the third shall be left therein.

Without getting into the specifics concerning the coming world leader, clearly anti-Semitism will be one of his secret doctrines, though he may arrive on the scene as a pseudo-Zionist. Prophetically, he must allow the re-building of the Jewish Temple. In so doing it may appear as though he has achieved the long-awaited peace in the Middle East. However, the coming world leader will eventually begin to exude a spirit of anti-Semitism that will dwarf past Crusades, Inquisitions, Pogroms, Holocausts, and Jihads. Whether he will be connected to Islam, apostate Christianity, or both remains to be seen. But one thing is clear, the coming antichrist will hate the Jews and he will likely persuade the world to do the same by espousing some degenerate form of Replacement Theology.

Conclusion

Satan will employ every resource at his disposal towards the destruction of the Jewish people, but ultimately his efforts will not succeed. The Lord has already set aside for Himself a remnant (Zechariah 12:10, 13:9; Matthew 23:39; Romans 11:26; Revelation 7:4, etc.), and that which He has spoken shall not return unto Him void. As Christians, we are in the midst of concentrated Spiritual warfare. We are called to stand against the wiles of the Devil and to not be ignorant of his devices. Let us endeavor to expose misguided attempts to theologically justify anti-Semitism through the deception that is Replacement Theology. Psalm 102:16:

When the LORD shall build up Zion, he shall appear in his glory.

[End of essay]

Note

In 2011 I helped to edit the book *When the Cross Became a Sword* by Merrill Bolender. This book has sold several thousand copies worldwide and has been translated into a half a dozen languages. Here is a product description I wrote for that important work:

> Merrill Bolender's *When The Cross Became a Sword* takes a timely look at an important topic. This 80 page book shines the spotlight on neglected chapters of the Church's untold past, with shocking results. Tracing back through nearly 2,000 years of ecclesiastical history, Merrill documents a troubling and tragic trend—Jewish blood on Christian hands. Even more fundamentally, *When The Cross Became a Sword* identifies Replacement Theology as the root cause of unspeakable evil perpetrated against God's chosen people. Arguing for the authority of God's Word and solid principles of Biblical interpretation, Merrill calls the Church to rediscover and embrace her Jewish roots. He rightly asserts that this is the only way Christians can avoid repeating the sins of the past.

This book is available through my website, www.scottkeisler.com.

So, what have we learned from all of this talk about Covenants and Israel? Let's take a look at *The Omega Manifesto* once again:

17) God unilaterally and unconditionally instituted the Abrahamic Covenant.

18) The Law of Moses (The Mosaic Covenant) was an imperfect and temporary covenant which pointed forward to Christ and the New Covenant.

19) Like the Mosaic Covenant, the New Covenant is to be seen within the broader context of the Abrahamic Covenant—the implication being that the New Covenant in no way replaces the Abrahamic Covenant.

20) The existence of the modern state of Israel is prophetically significant and points forward to the fulfillment of Daniel's 70th Week (a seven year period).

21) The Church does not replace Israel in God's plan for man.

22) The Church has sinned against Israel and the Jewish people throughout its history—the Body of Christ must repent if she is to avoid committing the same sins again in the future.

Endnotes for Replacement Theology Paper

(1) Dr. Thomas Ice, *What is Replacement Theology?* (Pre-Trib Research Center: 2003). http://www.pre-trib.org/article-view.php?id=249
(2) Bill Koenig: www.watch.org/showprint.php3?idx=64261&mcat=1&rtn=/index.html
(3) Ibid.
(4) Grant Jeffrey, *Prince of Darkness* (Toronto, Ontario: Frontier Research Publications, 1994), 127.
(5) Ice, *What is Replacement Theology?*
(6) Chuck Missler, *How to Study the Bible* (Koinonia House, 2006), MP3.
(7) Ibid.

(8) John Hagee, *Jerusalem Countdown* (Lake Mary, Florida: FrontLine, 2006), 73.

(9) Ice, *What is Replacement Theology?*.

(10) Chuck Missler, T*he Prodigal Heirs* (Koinonia House, 1995), 66/40 Radio Broadcast.

(11) Dave Hunt, *A Woman Rides the Beast* (Eugene, Oregon: Harvest House Publishers, 1994), 265.

(12) Ice, *What is Replacement Theology?*

(13) Dr. J. Randall Price, *Is the Modern State of Israel Prophetically Significant?* www.worldofthebible.com/Bible%20Studies/Is%20Israel%20Prophetically%20Significant.pdf

(14) Hunt, *Woman Rides Beast,* 292.

(15) www.pcusa.org/ga216/business/overtures/ovt0432.htm

(16) Jeffrey, *Prince of Darkness*, 127.

(17) www.state.gov/r/pa/prs/ps/2003/20062.htm

(18) Dr. Price, *Israel Prophetically Significant*

(19) Ibid.

(20) Dr. Thomas Ice, *Christian Zionism* (Pre-Trib Research Center: 2003).www.pre-trib.org/article-view.php?id=18

(21) Joel C. Rosenberg, *Epicenter* (Carol Stream, Illinois: Tyndale House Publishers, Inc., 2006), 26.

(22) Jeffrey, Prince of Darkness, 127.

(23) Ice, *What is Replacement Theology?*

(24) Dave Hunt, The Kingdom of God: www.thebereancall.org/Newsletter/html/1988/sep88.php

(25) Dave Hunt, Jews, Gentiles & the Church: www.thebereancall.org/Newsletter/html/1989/sep89.php

(26) Hal Lindsey, *The Late Great Planet Earth* (Grand Rapids, Michigan: Zondervan, 1970), 48-49.

(27) Dr. Dwight Pentecost, *The Relationship of the Church to the Kingdom of God* (Pre-Trib Research Center: 2003). www.pre-trib.org/article-view.php?id=98

(28) E. W. Bullinger, *The Witness of the Stars* (Grand Rapids, Michigan: Kregal Publications, 1893), 184.

(29) Ibid., 191.

(30) Rabbi Jeff Adler, response to personal email.

(31) Hal Lindsey, *The Everlasting Hatred*, the Roots of Jihad (Murrieta, California: Oracle House Publishing, 2002), 45.

(32) Ibid., 125.

Chapter 6—The Old World Order

What is the New World order? Who is the nebulous "they" those conspiracy theorists are always fretting about? Is there really a tiny group of extremely powerful individuals conspiring to take over the world? This chapter will sort fact from fiction and separate reality from theory. It will also provide a concise overview of the spiritual, political, and economic history of the New World Order. By standing back and taking in the big picture, and by connecting certain key dots, the reader will begin to understand that the New World Order is not some nebulous thought subsisting in the dark recesses of a paranoid imagination, it is a war being aggressively waged against humanity by global elites who often hide their schemes in plain view.

Like Truman in *The Truman Show*, humanity lives in a reality that is highly manipulated and controlled. Most people live their lives never suspecting that they are being systematically deprived of resources, information, and liberty. But once the facade of Truman's fake world had been compromised, Truman realized that evidence exposing the oppressive scheme had been hiding in plain view all along. Similarly, once an individual has been adequately deprogrammed, once they begin to realize that something is amiss, it becomes difficult to imagine how it was possible not to have seen the New World Order scam all along.

The Matrix is real. This book is a red pill, if you choose to accept it. Or you can choose to go on believing what you want to believe. The choice is yours.[1]

---

[5]The Matrix is a film that promotes Gnosticism, a view that I certainly don't endorse. This is merely an example borrowed from popular culture to illustrate a point.

For as long as humanity has inhabited planet earth, a class of ruling elites has sought to enslave the masses by systematically consolidating their power. From Alexander the Great to Caesar, from Napoleon to Hitler, would-be global despots have fantasized about ruling the world. Some historians have observed that the history of Europe can be rightly seen as a series of nations each taking its respective shot at global conquest. But let us start by going back—way back—to where it all began.

Ancient Desire

Historically, the first individual to attempt the mother of all power-grabs was Nimrod. More than 4,000 years ago in the period following the great flood, Noah's great grandson Nimrod emerged as a powerful leader. Not a great deal is known about Nimrod, but what is clear is that he was a man of great military prowess. Nimrod also shrewdly used spirituality as a means of uniting his people. Within just four generations of the flood, under their larger than life leader, the ancient people of Babel rebelled against God. Their rebellion was embodied in the construction of the Tower of Babel, a mystical tower that had a temple at the top where priests practiced idolatry and sorcery. The Tower and its religious system were doubtless central in the life of the people's city.

Nimrod's wife Semiramis was a priestess in the false religious system and she claimed to have given birth to a son without a human father. In ancient cultures Nimrod himself was deified and worshiped in various forms, including as a calf, a bull, a serpent, and a dragon. This pagan Babylonian system is extremely important because it served as the foundation for all of the ancient Mystery Religions, including (but not limited to) those of ancient Sumeria, Egypt, Persia, India, Greece, and Rome. These Mystery Religions were always hierarchical in nature and the secret doctrines they contained were commonly withheld from all but the highest level of inner circle adepts or initiates. Their practices were extremely occultic in nature.

God judged Nimrod and the Tower of Babel rebellion by confusing the languages and scattering the people all over the globe. (If this sounds implausible to you, consider the fact that secular ethnologists today will tell you that all languages seem to have derived from a single ancient ancestor.) Bits and pieces of Nimrod's religious system were preserved in the various indigenous religions around the world, especially in the Egyptians mysteries of Osiris, in Zoroastrianism, and in Hinduism. Ancient priesthoods sprang into existence and an inner circle of occult adepts carefully maintained and guarded the esoteric knowledge down through the ages. What is extremely interesting, much of this esoteric knowledge was preserved in the ancient civilizations of North America, Meso-America, and South America, as well as in the Druidic societies of Western Europe.

A few centuries passed and the secret doctrines of the Mystery Religions managed to successfully infiltrate Old Testament Judaism even as God began to reveal His plan for man through ancient Israel. This is highly significant. The result was Kabalism or the Kabala, a mystical, occult perversion of Biblical Judaism. Using the Truths of the Old Testament as a jumping off point—truths which they of course perverted—the Mystery Religions managed to give themselves a philosophical boost. Note that this is what evil must always do—vampirically and uncreatively leech off of good. In entertainment and pop culture, evil is presented as exciting, dynamic, and creative, but this is propaganda. In reality evil is dull, repetitious, and profoundly uncreative.

During the New Testament era, the Gnostics drew from their knowledge of the Kabalah and Greek Philosophy. Eventually they successfully mingled their ideas with a perverted reading of the Gospels and the Apostolic letters. As Gary Kah points out in his classic work, *En Route to Global Occupation*, the Kabalah and Gnosticism essentially form an occult version of the Old and New Testaments. Piggybacking off of (and perverting) the truths of God's Word while preserving the ancient mysteries, the Kabala and Gnosticism form the foundation of modern Western occultism.

Continuing our ancient story, during medieval times the Roman Catholic Church, seeking credibility in the world, "Christianized" many of the pagan beliefs of Rome, even incorporating some of the practices of the ancient Mystery Religions—but only to a point. At the same time, as the Roman Church came to power in Europe, many of the occult orders were forced underground.

Intriguingly, during Medieval times the Knights Templars, a military and religious order of the Catholic Church, began to study the Kabalah and Gnosticism. Aside from their exploits perpetrated during the Papal Crusades, the Templars became extremely wealthy international bankers and operated essentially as a tax free organization. This arrangement served as a model that the New World Order continues to use to this day. The Templars planned to use their wealth to buy power and influence in Europe—and eventually the rest of the world. In the Templars we see the first hard evidence of a merger between occult secret societies and international bankers. We also see the evidence of a plot to create a New World Order—not that they would have used that terminology. Eventually the Templar scheme was uncovered and the Church of Rome turned on them. Under the duress of extreme torture many Knights confessed to being Luciferians.

Many students of the esoteric point to this fact and argue that the Knights Templars were likely *not* Luciferians, rightly noting that those being tortured will confess to just about anything. However, in this case I am not so quick to buy into the idea of contrived confessions, as it is widely known that Lucifer is the light of the Kabalah, which the Templars were known to have practiced. (Albert Pike also tells us that Lucifer is the light of Freemasonry in *Morals and Dogma*.) In fact, my personal definition of the Illuminati is this:

> Those who sit atop the New World Order power structure, acting on behalf of "Lucifer" (Satan) to bring about a global government and a new world religion that will serve Satan's false messiah.

Recall Jesus' temptation in the wilderness where Satan offered Jesus all the kingdoms of this world in all their glory, if He would bow down and worship Satan. Jesus did not challenge Satan's authority to offer these kingdoms. Why? Because the Bible says that Satan is the present "god of this world." (Authority over the earth was originally given to Adam and Eve, but that authority was usurped by Satan in the Garden of Eden when Adam ate of the tree of the knowledge of good and evil.) The clear implication then, is that Satan had (and has) the ability to deliver the goods. In exchange for wealth and power, men can of their own free will and volition choose to serve Satan's larger agenda.

Were the Knights Templars Luciferians seeking to subdue the kingdoms of the world on behalf of Satan, the fallen archangel? One thing is for certain, the Knights Templars—at least those who weren't executed—were forced to go underground, along with their mystical beliefs and schemes of world domination.

Their teachings and occult practices were subsequently absorbed and preserved by another secret order known as the Rosicrucians. In the preface to Tom Horn's book, *Apollyon Rising 2012*, Chris Pinto specifically asserts that the Knights Templars fled to Scotland following their persecution in Europe. Is the Templar red cross the source of the Rosicrucian rose cross? We know that Scottish Freemasons built Rosslyn Chapel in 1492 and that eventually Rosicrucian doctrines were woven into Freemasonry (i.e. the Scotish Rite) under the supervision of Francis Bacon. This important merger of Masonry and Rosicrucianism laid the foundation for modern day Freemasonry. In fact, it is probable that the Rosicrucians became the initial adepts (occult masters) atop the hierarchical structure of Freemasonry. In other words, the Rosicrucians were the illuminated Masons sitting atop of the pyramid of power within the lodge.

To summarize thus far, we have learned that the essence of the ancient Mystery Religions has been preserved in the Eastern Religions, the Kabalah, Gnosticism, Roman Catholicism, and Illuminized Freemasonry (by way of the Knights Templars and the Rosicrucians). We also see the influence of the Mystery Religions in the Druids and the indigenous religions of the Americas.

Our narrative now arrives at one Adam Weishaupt. Adam Weishaupt wanted to start an order within an order and to embed it within the hierarchy of the Masonic Lodge. A prominent Mason himself, the purpose of Weishapt's new secret order, the administrative structure of which was modeled after the Jesuit Order, was to abolish Christianity and overturn all civil government. The Order came to be known as the Illuminati. Only a select few Masons—namely those who showed a proclivity towards the mystical and the occult—would be selected as initiates to go down the secretive path. The secretive path would be concealed behind the outer court of the lodge—the order of Masonry that is generally well-known. (Plus lower level Masons don't know what goes on in higher level Masonry anyway.) In other words, it is obvious that the aforementioned Illuminized Masons comprised Weishaupt's order within an order, the Illuminati.

Illuminati operatives successfully created an alliance with the powerful Rothschild Bankers of Europe. (Again note this important arrangement.) Weishaupt, like the Templars, was consciously laying the foundation for establishing a New World Order. The timing, interestingly enough, corresponded to the founding of America. (My position is that the founding of America was neither a wholly Christian endeavor, nor entirely the work of occult secret societies. I view America's founding fathers as a mixed bag, although publicly a strong Judea-Christian philosophical base was put forth.)

Fortunately, the subversive activities of the Bavarian Illuminati were discovered and exposed. Unfortunately, the order was never adequately eradicated. Long story short, the Grand Orient Lodge of France became one of the great guardians of Illuminized Freemasonry.

This brings us to Cecil John Rhodes. Rhodes was turned on to occult teachings by his Oxford professor and mentor

John Ruskin. Rhodes (after whom the Rhodes Scholarships are named) went on to amass one of the great fortunes in the history of the world. Using exploitation and political intrigue, Rhodes amassed untold millions in the diamond and gold mines of South Africa. He was a ruthless man who, like Weishaupt, forged an alliance with the Rothschild bankers. Gary Kah rightly points out in *En Route to Global Occupation* that both Rhodes and the Rothschild clans benefited from this relationship. Rhodes' secret societies benefited from the financing of the Rothschilds, while the Rothschilds benefited from the extensive political and business connections provided by the secret societies.

Rhodes created his secret societies (which, like Weishaupt, he modeled after the Jesuit Order) for the express purpose of taking over the world through the agency of the British government. Absurd as the idea may have sounded, Rhodes had a fabulous fortune and elite connections. Rhodes formed roundtable groups that became the predecessors of the Royal Institute of International Affairs in Great Britain. Energized by esoteric occult forces and financed by European Black Nobility Oligarchs, Rhodes' group quickly became nothing short of the shadow government operating just behind the curtain of the British Empire. By allying themselves with the International Bankers, and by using their wealth and influence to buy off politicians, the Milner Roundtable Groups (as they came to be known, named for Lord Alfred Milner who helped to execute Rhodes' plan) slowly gained control of strategic national and international centers of power. This essentially brings our story all the way up to WWI, where the plot really begins to thicken.

Puppetmasters Do America

Agents of the British roundtable groups crossed the pond and began establishing their puppet government structure here in the United States. Operating behind the scenes, agents of London's shadow government had perfected their covert techniques while extending the British Empire. Two of the foundation stones in their take-over scheme in the United States were the Federal Reserve and the Council on Foreign Relations. We will examine the Federal Reserve in this chapter.

The Federal Reserve

The creation of the Federal Reserve was one of the greatest scams in American history. It was also, as we shall see, a watershed moment in the push for world government. According to G. Edward Griffin, author of the essential work *The Creature from Jekyll Island*, the bankers who met in secret at J. P. Morgan's private retreat in Georgia represented between one-sixth and one-fourth of the *world's* wealth. (Griffin even states that these numbers could be conservative!) These bankers represented not only the money trust of Wall Street, including the Morgan and Rockefeller dynasties, but they also represented old world European money, the British, and the Rothschilds.

Paul Warburg of Kuhn, Loeb & Company is widely considered to have been the chief architect of the Federal Reserve system, which he modeled after that which was already in place in Europe—especially in Germany and the Bank of England. Having worked in Europe for much of his life, Warburg represented the Rothschilds at the Jekyll Island meeting. He went on to become the first Chairman of the Federal Reserve. Also present at the secretive Jekyll Island meeting were Rhode Island Senator Nelson Aldridge, who was intimately connected to J. P. Morgan (who himself was an agent of the Rothschilds). Senator Aldridge was also the Father-in-Law of John D. Rockefeller, Junior. Frank A. Vanderlip, President of the powerful Rockefeller National City of New York (Bank) was also in attendance. When you look at the players involved, the Jekyll Island scheme seems to have practically been a Rothschild-Rockefeller joint venture!

Though the banksters (as I will call them from here on out) of the Jekyll Island club were already fabulously wealthy, they weren't satisfied. The banking environment of early 20th century America was increasingly not to their liking. Here's why. Government regulations and subsidies permitted banks to back their money with only 10 percent gold. While this benefited the banksters, it also enabled other independent banks to create waves of easy currency. As a result, in the period right before the creation of the Federal Reserve system, independent banks were popping up everywhere and the banksters of the Wall Street-Washington establishment were steadily losing market share. For the banksters, there was too much competition! To industrialists like John D. Rockefeller and the finance oligarchs, this competition was seen as a sin. As G. Edward Griffin skillfully points out:

> Competition also was coming from a new trend in industry to finance future growth out of profit rather than from borrowed capital. This was the outgrowth of free-market interest rates which set a realistic balance between debt and thrift. Rates were low enough to attract serious borrowers who were confident of the success of their business ventures and of their

ability to repay, but they were high enough to discourage loans for frivolous ventures or those for which there were alternative sources of funding—for example one's own capital. The balance between debt and thrift was the result of a limited money supply. Banks could create loans in excess of their actual deposits, as we shall see, but there was a *limit* to that process. And that limit was ultimately determined by the supply of gold they held. Consequently, between 1900 and 1910, seventy per cent of the funding for American corporate growth was generated internally, making industry increasingly independent of the banks. Even the federal government was becoming thrifty. It had a growing stockpile of gold, was systematically redeeming the Greenbacks—which had been issued during the Civil War—and was rapidly reducing the national debt.(1)

Between the growing number of independent banks and the trend to finance expansion out of capital reserves, this state of affairs was unacceptable! Banksters, after all, make their money by making loans. Plus, on top of all of this, many of the greedier banks of the day were going bankrupt because they simply pushed the envelope too far in terms of loaning out their currency reserves. Put simply, when too many account holders and/or other banks came looking for cash (bank runs and currency drains), the money simply wasn't there because it had all been loaned out!

Scheming banksters desired an industry wide currency reserve standard—a market intervention that would lead to artificially low interest rates while effectively ending true competition. Such an arrangement would make loans more attractive while significantly mitigating the prospect of individual bank failures. But what if the banksters could achieve this feat *and* increase the money supply? What if the banksters had the ability to create almost infinite quantities of fiat cash? Why, it would be a banksters paradise!

This is exactly what the Jekyll Island club set out to do. But neither the public nor the Congress would ever go for it . . . unless the scheme could somehow be packaged as protecting the public while "stabilizing" Mr. Market! (Volatility was of course blamed on free markets, even though the banking industry was already regulated to a great extent.) This ploy of positioning their plan as protecting the public is precisely what was adopted.

But there was one further detail in the scheme that was the *real* kicker. What if the entire banking industry were to get drunk while riding a tidal wave of fiat currency? What if the entire industry were to become reckless and fail? What if the banksters could somehow get the Federal Government to sign on to the scheme, essentially making the American tax payer the "lender of last resort"? Or to put it in today's language, what if the banksters said they were too big to fail and needed a bailout to prevent financial armageddon?

Over the next three years the patient and resourceful banksters out-foxed Congress and the American people by employing the following strategy (I again defer to G. Edward Griffin):

1) Do not call [the Jekyll Island Plan] a cartel nor even a central bank.
2) Make it look like a government agency.

3) Establish regional branches to create the appearance of decentralization, not dominated by Wall Street banks.
4) Begin with a conservative structure including many sound banking principles knowing that the provisions can be quietly altered or removed in subsequent years.
5) Use the anger caused by recent panics and bank failures to create popular demand for monetary reform.
6) Offer the Jekyll Island Plan as though it were in response to that need.
7) Employ university professors to give the plan the appearance of academic approval.
8) Speak out *against* the plan to convince the public that Wall Street bankers do not want it.(2)

The strategy worked and in 1913 The Federal Reserve Act (The Glass-Owen Bill) was passed just before Christmas, when many of the Congressmen had already departed Washington for the holiday. The Federal Reserve system is a shared monopoly, a private bankster cartel that masquerades as a government agency. The Fed is unconstitutional and illegal, according to Article 1 Section 8 of the US Constitution. According to the Constitution, the power of the purse is to be delegated to the Congress and was never intended to be outsourced at interest to a bunch of international banksters who literally operate above the law.

There will be those, of course, who argue against this "conspiratorial" interpretation of history. The question of intent, however, is in at least one sense academic. Even if we [foolishly] grant that the original intent behind the creation of the Fed was in fact protecting the American public and stabilizing the market, we must admit that, in terms of these aims the Fed has been a catastrophic failure. As G. Edward Griffin puts it:

> "Since its inception, [the Fed] has presided over the crashes of 1921 and 1929; the Great Depression of '29 to '39; recessions in '53, '57, '69, '75, and '81; a stock market 'Black Monday' in '87; and a 1000% inflation which has destroyed 90% of the dollar's purchasing power."(3)

On the other hand, confronting the question of intent is absolutely essential. Was part of the reasoning behind the Fed the creation of a one world government? Are the powers behind the Fed committed to bringing down the United States? We will look at these questions in the next chapter, but the answer to this question is an obvious yes.

So what have we learned in terms of *The Omega Manifesto*?

23) There is nothing new about the New World Order, which goes all the way back to the political and religious system of ancient Babel.
24) The mystical essence of that system was preserved in the Mystery Religions and occult secret societies down through the ages.
25) The Illuminati are those who are consciously working on behalf of Lucifer to bring about global government and a one world religion that will serve Satan's false messiah.

26) The Federal Reserve system is the economic mechanism that has been used in America and around the world to build the New World Order.

Chapter 6 Endnotes

(1) G. Edward Griffin, *The Creature from Jekyll Island*, 12-13.
(2) Ibid., 438.
(3) Ibid., 20.

See also *En Route to Global Occupation*, by Gary Kah (especially chapter five), and *Brotherhood of Darknewss*, by Dr. Stanley Monteith.

Chapter 7—The New World Order

In the previous chapter I asserted that the creation of the Federal Reserve represented a major tipping point in the move towards global government. But this event did not occur in a cultural vacuum. By the end of the 19th century the Industrial Revolution was in full bloom and populations in US cities began to boom. The growth occurred so fast, in fact, that it began to put a strain on infrastructure demands. Up until this time, Americans had a reputation for being independent and individualistic. The idea of limited central government was widely accepted as an American value. But as the 20th century dawned there was an increasing willingness for government to play a larger role in American life. Additionally, at about the same time the Federal Reserve Act was passing, the ideas of the European Enlightenment began to take root in the United States. The change began in academia and filtered its way slowly down into the culture at large. Humanism began to undercut the Judea-Christian base and collectivism began the slow process of replacing American individualism.

By 1917 the US had entered World War I, coming to the aid of the British and their banking overlords. Incidentally, the same banksters behind the Federal Reserve are now known to have bankrolled the Bolshevik Revolution (also in 1917). After the Russian Revolution the money powers enjoyed a cozy (and profitable) relationship with the new Russian government—which would go on to slaughter as many as 60 million before all was said and done.

As it drew to a close, World War I was dubbed the war to end all wars as at least 20 million people worldwide were killed during the conflict. Following World War I an attempt at an upstart world government failed in the League of Nations, which the United States refused to join.

The Council on Foreign Relations

In 1919, the exact same powers behind the creation of the Federal Reserve (Banksters and secret societies) began the process of creating the Council on Foreign Relations—the Rothschilds, Rockefellers, Warburgs, Morgans, etc. Formally launched in 1921, the Council on Foreign Relations was the American manifestation of a growing block of Fabian Socialists in New York, Washington, and London. Fabian Socialism, a humanistic political outlook that operates on the base of the Hegelian Dialectic, seeks to slowly infiltrate and take over key cultural institutions. In other words, this brand of socialism is a slow revolution that takes place via a march through the culture. This in contrast with the Marxists, who as John Loeffler puts it are socialists in a hurry with a gun. The Council on Foreign Relations set out to create international economic structures that would eventually override national arrangements. Or, said another way, the CFR wanted to undermine American sovereignty in such a way that eventually the implementation of a supra-national world government would seem quite natural. America emerged from World War I as the undisputed superpower in the world (though technically the British Empire peaked in the '20s). Elites of the bankster-CFR establishment have used America's power and might since that time to do the grunt work of building the New World Order. Don't be fooled by this arrangement however. When the jig is up and the NWO is complete, America must no longer remain a world superpower. Just over a decade ago this statement seemed improbable, but we are already witnessing signs that the days of America's dominance on the world stage are drawing to a close. Chief among these signs is the decline of the dollar. A complete economic collapse could be imminent, but more on that later.

The CFR received funding from foundations like the and Carnegie Foundations—which are tax exempt "think tanks" that serve as crucial policy makers for the shadow government. CFR white papers, which can be read in the organization's publication *Foreign Affairs*, have a strange way of becoming official US policy. The CFR has dominated Presidential administrations since the days of F. D. R. The CFR has also dominated both the Democratic and Republican parties for decades. The idea of a truly democratic process in America has been an illusion for quite a long time. As F. D. R. said, Presidents are selected, not elected.

The CFR also controls the State Department, the Department of Defense, the Treasury and so on. Put simply, the CFR *is* the shadow government in the United States. This fact is so easily verifiable that I will not devote any further time towards defending the assertion.

At the same time the banksters and their secret society friends were establishing the CFR in New York, they were setting up the Royal Institute of International Affairs (Chattam House) in London. The RIIA of course is the end result of the Milner Roundtable Groups established by Cecil Rhodes and company.

From the year 1921 to 1929, the American economy grew steadily and virtually uninterrupted. The banksters were pumping waves of fiat cash into the economy and the roaring 20's was the result. On the other side of the pond, however, the British economy was treading water. Incredibly, in *The Creature from Jekyll Island* G. Edward Griffin makes a solid case that the Stock Market crash of 1929 was deliberately engineered as a means of buoying the British economy.

By 1932 the Great Depression was in full swing and the crisis had prepared the masses for Franklin D. Roosevelt's New Deal. F. D. R., a 33rd degree Freemason and blood relative of the British Royal Family, convinced the Treasury to put the esoteric Great Seal on the US dollar bill. He also became the face of big government and socialism in America. His administration was the manifestation of the aforementioned Fabian Socialist bloc in the US and Great Britain. A few years later, F. D. R. and Winston Churchill would negotiate behind the scenes to get the United States involved in World War II. Meanwhile, the banksters of the Fed and the corporations which had grown up around them—the same bunch who had funded the Bolsheviks in 1917—began aiding Hitler's war effort. (This will be documented in the next chapter.)

The United Nations

In the days following World War II the planet witnessed the creation of the United Nations. As Gary Kah points out in *En Route to Global Occupation*,

> "CFR control of the State Department would ensure membership in the United Nations following the war. In fact, the Council on Foreign Relations would act through the State Department to establish the UN."[1]

The US had refused to join the League of Nations following World War I, effectively killing that adventure before it ever got off the ground. This time the globalists of the American shadow government would not be denied. Ten of the 14 members on the committee which planned the UN and its charter were CFR members while 47 members of the US delegation at the UN's founding conference were members of the Council on Foreign Relations.(2) To sweeten the deal for hesitant Americans, the UN building would be built on US soil—on grounds donated by John D. Rockefeller, Jr. The UN was to serve as a form of limited world government, with particular emphasis on policing the third world.

I personally loathe the UN with all of my being. It is the most corrupt, inept, and hypocritical organization in the history of mankind. It is a breeding ground for bizarre alternative spirituality, pseudo intellectualism, and elitism that is completely detached from reality. The UN literally commits genocide while positioning itself as a loving bunch of compassion-filled humanitarians. Their agents rape, rob, and kill with diplomatic immunity while celebrities like Bono have shameless benefit concerts that indoctrinate the youth with pro-UN propaganda. It's disgusting! It makes me want to throw up. But when some talking-head from the corporate whore media gets on TV and talks about how wonderful the UN is, the average American buys it hook, line, and sinker.

Programmed

Speaking of talking-heads, let's go down that rabbit hole for a moment. Radio, TV, and film were never intended to be simply forms of entertainment. Social engineers quickly recognized the power of media and set out to harness its potential. The word for media literally comes from a Persian word which roughly translates as sorcery. TV sure does seem to cast a spell on people. The flicker rate of the television (which produces 30 images per second) induces a hypnotic-like alpha state in the individual watching. Literally it's a near sleep state. In TV shows and programs, social messages can be delivered, not through logical or factual sequences, but through emotive sequences which intentionally end run one's reason. This is a powerful way to engineer social change. They are called TV programs because that's exactly what is happening—the viewer is being programmed!

The news media pride themselves not on informing public opinion, but in *forming* public opinion. They authoritatively present us with prepackaged ideas and conclusions that we tend to uncritically accept as reality. They often fail to tell us the whole story by leaving out key facts. And what they do tell us is often politicized and put through the spin-cycle. As astute readers will have noticed, the media, especially MSNBC (which is openly run by a White House front group funded by George Soros), are fond of playing the race and class cards. Why? A public that is busy fighting each other is less likely to organize against the establishment and is more easily manipulated and "moved" towards a desired social outcome via the Dialectical process.

I'm not saying it is bad to watch a TV program or to go to a (decent) movie. But I am saying don't drop your guard when you go. Realize that destructive social messages and a pro New World Order philosophy are almost always being pushed on you. (That philosophy is usually globalism, collectivism, materialistic Humanism, and/or some form of mystical spirituality.) Also realize that a news story is seldom ever just a news story. There is almost always an agenda behind the story, or at the very least a political spin factor contained within. People who say, "It's just a movie" or "It's just a TV show" are woefully (or willfully) ignorant. I know it is unbelievable but it has gotten so bad that any time we read a mainstream news article we need to ask ourselves, what is the government trying to sell me here?

Bilderberg and the Trilateral Commission

In 1954 the world saw the first Bilderberg conference. Bilderberg is an annual conference attended by the who's who of international finance, industry, politics, military, and media, and the result of their "conversations" go a long way towards determining the global agenda for the subsequent 12 months. Established in 1954 by Holland's Prince Bernhard, a high ranking Nazi SS officer with close ties to Royal Dutch Shell and the World Wildlife Fund, Bilderberg was nurtured into being by British MI6 under the direction of the Royal Institute of International Affairs.(3) The directorates of Bilderberg, RIIA, and other sister organizations like the Council on Foreign Relations are interlocking and, as we've already seen, essentially serve as shadow governments in the US, the UK, Europe and beyond.

Funded (once again) by tax exempt think tanks like the Rockefeller and Ford Foundations, Bilderberg's initial charge was the political and economic integration of Europe.(4) Under the Trojan horse of trade agreements like the European Coal and Steel Community, Bilderberg set out to create a European Superstate—a United States of Europe. That this was the agenda all along is evidenced by a document that came out of the 1957 Bilderberg conference:

". . . The discussion affirmed complete support for the idea of integration and unification from the representatives of all the six nations of the Coal and Steel Community present at the conference. . . . [There was] some expression by certain European participants of the view that in the economic field, it might be better to proceed through the development of a common market. . . . A European speaker expressed concern about the need to achieve a common currency, and indicated that in his view this necessarily implied the creation of a central political authority."(5)

This is, of course, exactly what eventually happened. The Coal and Steel Community gave way to the European Economic Community, which in turn gave way to the European Union and the creation of the single currency for the whole of Europe—the Euro.

The Bilderberg conference rotates each year between Europe, Asia, and North America, the three regions which are being progressively integrated economically via the Trilateral Commission (created in 1973 by David Rockefeller and Zbigniew Brzezinski). Global elites have been largely successful in creating their European Superstate, and now they have turned their attentions to creating similar North American and Asian Unions.

In North America, NAFTA and GATT (which Al Gore crammed down the American people's throat) established the Trojan horse trade ties that had already been tested and tried in Europe. Once these free trade agreements (which are actually subsidized trade agreements) had adequately developed, it was time to green light the Security and Prosperity Partnership. A 2005 conference held at Baylor University created this vehicle for political integration without consulting the will of the American people—indeed in spite of the will of the American people. The Security and Prosperity Partnership, on a continent wide level, regulates transportation, construction, manufacturing, banking, education, agriculture, law enforcement, and even the military. The proposed Trans NAFTA Super Highway and the Trans Texas Corridor would go a long way towards making such integration possible while generating enormous revenue for the New World Order. It is already the case that the Chinese can unload their cargo on the Pacific Coast of Southern Mexico. That cargo then travels, duty free, by rail to Kansas City, Missouri, where Mexico has an inland port that is considered the sovereign territory of Mexico. The creation of a North American superstate has evidently been fast-tracked.

The foundation for a similar Asian Union has been laid in the APEC and ASEAN trade agreements. Once the task of creating European, North American, and Asian superstates is completed, the three superstates will be merged and the resulting megalith will serve as the foundation of a truly world government (with the UN policing the third world). Incredibly, there are already signs that this phase is underway. The Transatlantic Economic Council has been charged with the integration of the European Union and the would-be American Union. This TEC council has already begun the task of regulating intellectual property, education, mergers and acquisitions, the military, and eventually Carbon Taxes and Cap and Trade—which will be paid to Al Gore . . . literally. Incredibly, there is also a Trans-Pacific Partnership in place that is moving towards the integration of the economies of North and South America, Asia, Australia, and New Zealand. Obviously the processes are ongoing, but it is amazing to see so much happening so quickly with few Americans aware of what is actually going on—the literal merger of European, American, and Asian Superstates.

To this global end, Bilderbergers meet in secret and behind closed doors to plan, scheme, and coordinate. Importantly, under the Logan Act it is illegal for those currently holding political office in the United States to attend such secret meetings without the express authority of the US government, due to the obvious conflicts of interests which can arise when politicians meet privately with foreign financiers, industrialists, and technocrats.

Not surprisingly, media moguls (often CFR members) also attend the annual global confab, but until recently they executed a complete media blackout, even denying the very existence of Bilderberg—mocking those who exposed the scheme as conspiracy theorists having hallucinations.

David Rockefeller relishes this complete lack of transparency, gloating at Bilderberg '91:

> "We are grateful to *The Washington Post*, *The New York Times*, *Time Magazine* and other great publications whose directors have attended our meetings and respected their promises of discretion for almost forty years. . . . It would have been impossible for us to develop our plan for the world if we had been subjected to the lights of publicity during those years. But, the world is more sophisticated and prepared to march towards a world government. The supranational sovereignty of an intellectual elite and world bankers is surely preferable to the national auto-determination practiced in past centuries."(6)

Incredibly, 90 percent of the CFR controlled corporate whore media is controlled by *six* companies—CBS, Disney, GE, News-Corp, Time Warner, and Viacom. By controlling these companies, the CFR own the media and control the flow of information (and disinformation). For the Democratic dupes, CNN and MSNBC spin to the left. For the war-mongering neo-con types, FoxNews spins to the right. The partisan pundits and the talking-heads bicker viciously over superficial details and contrived talking points as they engage in what Dr. Stanley Monteith terms political theater. On issues that really matter to the globalists, the Democrats and the Republicans stand absolutely united. The political reality of our day is a one party dictatorship that offers two "flavors" of tyranny. Sadly, lapdog journalists in the mainstream press form what amounts to a band of state run TV networks.

Revolution

Jumping back, by the 60s a very young and a very large generation of baby boomers was coming of age in America. The Humanism that began to manifest in the 20s and 30s among the elites had trickled down all the way through the culture. In 1962 school prayer was banned and in 1963 Bibles were kicked out of the public schools. The Beetles crossed the pond and their new brand of music was a form of cultural shock treatment that ignited an irreverent revolution of sex, drugs, and rock 'n' roll.

Yet just under the radar, few people realize that a British black magician and Satanist named Aleister Crowley can rightly be considered the father of modern culture (though he died in 1947). This is not a compliment. As skillfully documented in the 10 hour rockumentary *They Sold Their Souls for Rock 'n' Roll*, Crowley pioneered a brand of magick (he spelled it with a k) that taught people to get into contact with spiritual entities and demons. Chief among his methodologies were rituals involving sex and drugs. Many consider Crowley to be the true father of the New Age movement because in one of his most influential writings, *The Book of the Law*, he wrote of a coming New Aeon [Greek for Age] of Horus which would coincide with "the establishment on earth of a new order."[7] In esoteric lore, Horus is known as the Conquering Child and in Crowley's work Horus is an obvious allusion to the coming Biblical Antichrist. The Age of Aquarius then is a thinly veiled reference to Crowley's coming New Age of Antichrist.

Defunct Harvard Professor Timothy Leary, who felt that he was carrying Crowley's mantle, helped to introduced drug use into the hippie culture of the 60s. Leary is especially known for encouraging the use of LSD, which has been connected to MK-Ultra, the illegal mind control and brainwashing program run by the CIA and the British Tavistock Institute for Human Relations. (According to Wikipedia, Tavistock was initially funded by a grant from the Rockefeller Foundation.) Leary openly lauded Crowley and felt it was his life's calling to carry on his work.

Alfred Kinsey, who produced the fraudulent and skewed Kinsey Reports by using a sample population of prison inmate sex offenders, was obsessed with Crowley's homo-erotic poetry and a pervert of the highest order. Similarly, as a youth Harry Hay—widely considered the father of the modern homosexual movement—played the organ for the Ordo Templi Orientus (OTO), a Satanic order which was and is heavily influenced by the magick of Aleister Crowley. Hay practiced and taught workshops about sex magick rituals and often quoted Crowley in his work. Between Kinsey, Hay, and Kenneth Anger (who made the Satanic film *Lucifer Rising* that also involved the Rolling Stones entourage and Jimmy Page of Led Zeppelin), the foundation for the modern homosexual movement was laid. *Playboy* magazine credited Kinsey's phony research in its first issue while Robert Anton Wilson, long-time editor of the Playboy Forum, bragged about practicing Crowley's magick and reading all of his available works. Thus we see the direct influence of Crowleyan Satanism bubbling just under the surface of the sex and drugs of the 60s and 70s.

The hippie movement positioned itself as an anti-materialistic peace movement, but in reality it was a gateway that swung the door wide open not only for cultural destruction, but for demonic strongholds. One of Crowley's stated goals was the synthesis of Eastern Mysticism and Western Occultism. Crowley taught that one could become a musical genius by contacting the spirit world (demons and fallen angels). Harry Hay alluded to this by stating that "music always had the power to inspire revolt and revolution."[8] If you look at the biggest musical artists of all time, so many of them were and are practitioners and promoters of Crowleyan ideas. The Beetles, The Rolling Stones, Led Zeppelin, The Doors, The Eagles, Black Sabbath, David Bowie, Sting, The Cure, and Hall & Oates—sometimes subtly, sometimes overtly—all lauded (or laud) Crowley's magick in one way or another. The list could go on and on.

Corresponding precisely to the counterculture revolution that was unleashed in the 60s, America saw a dramatic increase in violent crime, divorce, sexually transmitted disease, and suicide while test scores and student achievement began plummeting. The fruit of this revolution has been nothing less than the destruction of our culture. This, of course, was the plan. Kick God out and replace him with a global regime—the New World Order and its occult messiah.

(Re)-Education

Let's go back and take a look at education in the United States of America during the same general period of time we've been covering in this chapter. Going back to as early as the 20s and 30s, the public school system in America began to be weaponized and used as an instrument of social revolution (by the Fabian Socialist / Progressive crowd). This is not a conspiracy. The agitators of this revolution openly telegraphed where they wanted to take our youth—arrogantly assuming the average person would never take the time to uncover their plan. Sadly, we must admit that they were correct in this regard.

The father of modern progressive education was undoubtedly John Dewey. In his early career, Dewey was a faculty member at the Rockefeller funded University of Chicago. During the period of 1910-1920, Dewey began to say that he wanted to take over public schools and to replace the Judea-Christian ethos in America with a humanistic ethos. Dewey, who along with Charles Francis Potter penned the Humanist Manifesto in 1933, played a key role in establishing the Teachers College at Columbia University as the hub of public school education in America. Dr. Dennis Cuddy, who was a Senior Associate at the US Department of Education in Washington, notes about the Teacher's College at Columbia:

"By the mid-1950s, this college was producing about one-third of the presidents and deans at accredited teacher training institutions, about 20 percent of all public school teachers, and over one-fourth of the superintendents of schools in the largest 168 cities in the US. By the early 1960s, Dewey's 'progressive' education was in almost every school in the land."(9)

Summing up the aims of progressive education, Humanist Manifesto co-author Charles Francis Potter crowed in 1930:

"Education is thus a most powerful ally of Humanism. What can the theistic Sunday schools, meeting for an hour once a week, and teaching only a fraction of the children, do to stem the tide of a five-day program of humanistic teaching?"(10)

Those, as they say, were fighting words, but the Church (and the culture at large) did next to nothing to take a stand for our children. Progressive educrats set out to, through incrementalism, systematically undermine moral abosolutes, individualism, and nationalism. They eradicated such 'traditional' values by teaching the students that they were (and are) morally autonomous decision-makers operating within a global collectivist paradigm.(11) Again I quote Dr. Cuddy's important article:

"Brock Chisholm (head of the World Health Organization and close friend of Communist spy Alger Hiss) published an article in the February 1946 edition of *PSYCHIATRY*, in which he revealed their strategy that 'a program of re-education or a new kind of education' needed to be charted to 'help our children to carry out their responsibilities as world citizens. . . . We have swallowed all manner of poisonous certainties fed us by our parents, our Sunday and day school teachers, our politicians, our priests. . . . The reinterpretation and eventual eradication of the concept of right and wrong. . . , the substitution of intelligent and rational thinking for faith in the certainties of old people, these are the belated objectives . . . for charting the changes in human behavior."(12)

This is all very clear. Nobody is mincing words. Having researched the global elites for nearly a decade, I can say with authority that this kind of candid rhetoric is not unusual. The assumption is made that the sheeple won't pay any attention.

In 1947, William Carr wrote an article for the National Education Association Journal entitled, *On the Waging of Peace*:

"As you teach about the United Nations, lay the ground for a stronger United Nations by developing in your students a sense of world community. The United Nations should be transformed into a limited world government. Teach those attitudes which will result ultimately in the creation of world citizenship and world government. We cannot directly teach loyalty to a society that does not exist, but we can and should teach those skills and attitudes which will help to create a society in which world citizenship is possible."(13)

Today, much of the education policy in the US comes down to the Department of Education via UNESCO, the UN organization that promoted Robert Muller's World Core curriculum (which incorporates flagrant occultism). In 1948 Julian Huxely of UNESCO wrote:

"The general philosophy of UNESCO should be a scientific world Humanism, global in extent, evolutionary in background. In its education program it can stress the ultimate need for world political unity and familiarize all people with the implications of the transfer of full sovereignty from separate nations to a world organization."(14)

Through education, children are being brainwashed into materialistic, evolutionary Humanism that is inherently anti-Christian, anti-Capitalism, and that undermines the role of the traditional family in society. While all of this is going on, our kids are being dumbed down deliberately! Before these guys (progressive educators) came along, education was based on facts, memorization, categorical thinking, and critical thinking. Tests essentially measured a student's knowledge. Today students are taught relativistic situational ethics (role playing) and through the Dialectical processes they are encouraged to focus on what they think and how they feel. In other words, within the broader context of the collective, they think with their feelings because moral categories are made to appear subjective, personal, and evolving. Today students take assessments (not tests) which psychologically profile the student and the extent to which he or she has integrated humanistic social norms into his or her worldview. The assessments serve as a feedback loop that tells the evaluators whether or not the student is politically correct in his views. (This is how mental health is now defined!)

In 1951, AH Loffner wrote an article entitled, *How Can the Junior High Curriculum Bbe Improved?*, in which he wrote:

"Three r's for all children, and all children for the three r's (reading, writing, and arithmetic). We've made some progress in getting rid of that slogan, but every now and then some mother with a Phi Beta Kappa award or some employer who has hired a girl who can't spell stirs up a fuss about the schools and progress is lost. When we come to the realization that not every child has to read, figure, write, and spell, that many of them either cannot or will not master these chores, then we shall be on the road to improving Junior High curriculum. For those thousands that have neither capacity nor desire to work in those areas, the school must provide other types of activities they can and will do. It's time for us to stop cramming these subject materials down all mouths—and I shall now include history and geography. Establish such flexibility in the curriculum as will permit realization of the dream and improvement will have come about."[15]

Quotes like these could be re-produced *ad nauseam*. Charlotte Iserbyt's seminal work *the deliberate dumbing down of america* is 800-plus pages of pure documentation. This book may be downloaded as a pdf file for free at www.deliberatedumbingdown.com. The bottom line is that, incrementally and piece mil, the humanistic agenda of progressive education has created a nationwide network of secular seminaries that absolutely push their worldview in the name of diversity, tolerance, and inclusion. Outcome Based Education, Goals 2000, and School to Work are all different program titles referring to different aspects of the same revolution. We can debate the fine details of these programs, but unless we step back and see them within the broader context of the overall agenda (and that's exactly what it is), we are spinning our wheels and wasting our time. Teachers (who usually have good intentions and sincere motives) have been indoctrinated into this way of thinking through the credentialing / licensing process. Those who think they can "do their own thing" in the classroom are sadly mistaken, because their outcomes either are or will be monitored and data-based. Those who don't tow the humanistic line will be removed. Apart from a full-scale national repentance, it would take 30 years to undo the damage that has been done by progressive education, even if we started today! People my age and younger have been absolutely sovietized. An ideological subversion has taken place. Of the demoralized masses, former KGB officer Yuri Bezmenov says of *our* students,

> "They are programmed to think and react to certain stimuli in a certain pattern. You cannot change their minds, even if you expose them to authentic information. Even if you prove that white is white and black is black, you still cannot change the basic perception and the logic of behavior."[16]

Through control of education, global elites shape the way we think (Dialectically, collectively, politically correctly). Through control of media, global elites fill our minds with disinfo, propaganda, and even destructive subliminal messages. (Note: like the average teacher, the average mid-level worker at CNN or FoxNews is not aware of the full agenda. Elites at the very top, however, know full-well what is going on.) The result of this assault on the American public is that the average individual lives in a false-reality matrix. Like a software update, those who are "plugged in" to this matrix of deception receive the same "upgrades" at the same time via the media.

False Flags

No "assessment" of the New World Order would be complete without a word on False Flag ops. The False Flag is a time-tested methodology in the playbook of tyranny that power-grabbing despots have turned to again and again down through history. The False Flag is often a self-inflicted wound that is blamed on a political enemy and exploited for political and economic purposes. Much of the info in this section comes from Alex Jones' film *Terror Storm*.

An ancient example is Nero, who set Rome on fire and blamed it on the Christians. Not so long ago, Nathan Roth-schild got word of Lord Wellington's victory over Napoleon almost a full day ahead of the "mainstream" channels. Roth-schild then put out a rumor that Napoleon had won, causing the stock market to plummet. Rothschild bought the sagging shares and when the word of the British victory arrived, stocks soared and Rothschild owned an enormous segment of the entire British economy having purchased his shares at rock bottom prices.(17)

But let's look at just a select few examples from modern times to get a further feel for how this works.

*1933—The Third Reich set fire to the Reichstag (parliament) building and blamed it on a mentally ill patsy. In the name of security, freedom gobbling measures similar to the US Patriot Act were implemented as the Nazi war machine powered up.

*1939—Operation Himmler blamed Poland for an attack on a German radio station near the Polish border, though the attack was actually carried out by a German prison inmate dressed up as a Polish soldier. The outraged German masses then supported the subsequent invasion of Poland.

*1953—Operation Ajax (declassified in 1990) begins in Iran. Funded by CIA director Allen Dulles (a finance oligarch and Nazi collaborator who also served as the President of the Council on Foreign Relations from 1946-1950), Operation Ajax overthrew the democratically elected pro-Western and anti-communist government of Mohammad Mossadegh in favor of the Shah. Mossadegh had refused to grant BP a monopoly over Persian (Iranian) oilfields. In response, elements of the CIA and MI6 (including Kermit Roosevelt, grandson of F. D. R.) orchestrated a series of false flags that were pinned on Mossadegh. For example, to cast Mossadegh in a negative light in order to weaken his administration, Western Intelligence staged demonstrations, executed bombings targeting mosques and religious leaders, machine-gunned civilians, and distributed propaganda leaflets saying "Up with Mossadegh, Up with Communism, Down with Allah." Once the Shah was installed, Nazi collaborator General Fazlollah Zahedi was put in as Prime Minister. Fazlollah "then signed twenty-five-year leases on forty percent of Iran's oil with three American companies, one of which was Gulf Oil, which a few years later named Kermit Roosevelt (F. D. R.'s grandson) as President!"(18)

*1947-1981—Operation Gladio was a blanket name for a series of subversive bombings carried out around the world perpetrated by Western Intelligence and elements of NATO. Buses, trains, and schools were specifically targeted. The deaths of innocent civilians were then blamed on leftists and communists.

*1964—The Gulf of Tonkin incident was supposedly carried out by hostile boats that attacked an American destroyer. However, this does was not the case. In November of 2001, tapes released by the L. B. J. Presidential Library Museum revealed conversations between L. B. J. and then Secretary of Defense Robert McNamara. The conversations make it clear that what ever happened was intended as a pretext to expand the war in Vietnam. Even the CIA's own official history (declassified in 2005) admits that "skewed intelligence" led to the deaths of over 58,000 Americans and 1.5 million Vietnamese.

*1967—The events surrounding the attack on the *USS Liberty* remain clouded in mystery to this day. According to some researchers, the attack on the US spy ship was to be blamed on Egypt as a pretext for the US entering the Six Day War, which would then expand to engulf much of the Middle East. Those who hold to this viewpoint assert that L. B. J. made a backroom deal with Israel, who sent three unmarked Mirage 3 fighter bombers to attack the *USS Liberty,* even though it was clearly marked and parked in international waters.

According to others, Israel's actions against the *Liberty* were designed to send Washington a strong signal to stay out of the burgeoning war (essentially to *prevent* it from expanding). Such a rebuke from one of America's strongest allies would have been a political disaster for the Johnson administration.

While it is unclear what happened, an obvious cover-up subsequently took place and we know for sure that L. B. J. actually ordered US fighters, which had been deployed to provide the *Liberty* with air support, to stand down. Multiple sources were on the line and heard the order. Fortunately, the Six Day War ended quickly (and miraculously) and establishment evil appears to have been largely thwarted.

911?

The 911 attacks on the WTC and the Pentagon have all the earmarks of a False Flag. NORAD stood down, and there is evidence that the Chairman of the Joint Chiefs and Dick Cheney were involved in the stand down order. WTC buildings 1, 2, and 7 appear to have been brought down via controlled demolition, with the media (including BBC) announcing that 7 had fallen an hour too early. Contained within the footprint of the WTC complex we have smoking-gun evidence of traces of a specific type of thermite used in controlled demolitions. Larry Silverstein, who leased the entire World Trade Center Complex, is on record saying that the order was given to "pull" (bring down) Building 7. Firefighters and police told crowds ahead of time that Building 7 was coming down. How in the world did they know that? It's not like an airplane hit that building. Many near all three buildings in New York reported having heard rapid sequential detonations characteristic of a controlled demolition.

Subsequent to 911 the US Patriot Act was passed (another tell-tale sign). In the name of security, individual liberties guaranteed by the Constitution of the United States have been eroded almost to the point of extinction. A massive and lucrative war with Iraq and Afghanistan followed, even though there was and is no direct link between those nations and 911.

Then we have the members of the 911 commission who have stated for the record that the "findings" of that document were a total sham. Why did that report not even *mention* Building 7? Two airplanes, one at the Pentagon and one in a Pennsylvania field magically disintegrated without a trace, yet in New York a terrorist passport was discovered perfectly intact just lying on the ground.

And on and on we could go. I'm not sure what happened on 911, but one thing *is* for sure. The official story is nonsense and our liberties have disappeared. Even more alarmingly, the apparatus of the international War on Terror is now turning inward as the Department of Homeland Security and FEMA prepare for civil unrest and Martial Law. Do they know something we don't?

Economic False Flag

In late 2008 and early 2009 the bottom dropped out of the American economy and a great recession began. The supposed cause of the meltdown was the failure of the sub-prime mortgage market. But what happened with the sub-prime market was a symptom, not a cause. I am not an economist and I don't even consider myself that knowledgeable when it comes to matters of finance and money. But I do know enough to know that the idiots who get on TV and talk about recovery are absolutely clueless as to what is actually going on. Either that or they are colluding. (Actually, some of it is frankly just wishful thinking—which goes back to what I said in the intro about normalcy bias and people not wanting to think about the unthinkable.) The sub-prime situation of 2008 was only the opening act of a broader financial storm that is coming our way. And what is coming will make the period between 2008 and now seem like the good old days. We are about to go off of a massive cliff at full throttle!

The creation of the Fed led to the ability to create fiat cash at will. The banksters loan us our own money at interest while those with direct access to the Fed system get the inside baseball on interest rates. (Plus they get the money before it trickles down through the economy, causing inflation—which is not technically prices going up but the value of the dollar going down due to the increase in the money supply.) The dollar was taken off the gold standard, partially at first and then completely with Richard Nixon, and so the money supply became theoretically infinite! Wall Street insiders and banksters create artificial fiat bubbles, the economy expands, and the good times roll. Periodically, however, the banksters cut off the money supply, the bubble pops, and the market goes down. Financial professionals know how to make money on the way down as well as on the way up, and when the market crashes they come in and buy shares on the cheap. The banksters have just sheered the American public. What's worse, with these enormous profits the powers that be buy up sectors of the economy not already under their control. Then they start pumping money into the economy again and the process repeats. This is how the banksters came to own the Fortune 500!

But note, this is *not* capitalism, as the Occupy Wall Street crowd mistakenly believes. This is corporatism, crony capitalism, or fascism, sitting atop a vampiric socialism—as Alex Jones has described. Conservatives foolishly defend the system as Capitalism while Liberals refuse to see that the very imperial corporations they decry are funding the supposedly benign socialism they champion. The idea that communism falls to the extreme left of the political spectrum and that fascism falls to the extreme right is another propaganda trick of the elites. The logical conclusion of communism and fascism is essentially the same (with minor differences). As Gary Allen puts it in his book *None Dare Call it a Conspiracy*:

> "The idea that socialism is a share-the-wealth program is strictly a confidence game to get the people to surrender their freedom to an all-powerful collectivist government. While the *Insiders* tell us we are building a paradise on earth, we are actually constructing a jail for ourselves." (emphasis in original)

And if the insiders are truly insiders, how then can you argue that they represent capitalism or free and fair markets? The answer is obviously that you cannot!

With the dollar off the gold standard, in the 1990s we saw the repeal of the Glass-Steagall Act. This was an important moment in our nation that I believe represents the greenlighting of the final take-down of the US economy. The Glass-Steagall Act of 1933 said there was an inherent conflict of interest between commercial banking and investment banking. A bank could be a commerical bank (like Chase) or an investment bank (like J. P. Morgan), but it could not be both. The repeal of Glass-Steagall did away with this prohibition. Now we have J. P. Morgan Chase—or as I like to call it, Rockefeller-Rothschild. Free to scheme and conflict of interests be damned, there soon developed new "financial products" called derivatives—which I'm not certain anyone fully understands. In the name of "market efficiency" and "the creative genius of Wall Street," these products create mechanisms for Accounting Control Fraud that allow for the creation of the biggest ponzi schemes in the history of mankind. But hey, the establishment said the products were safe and legitimate, so individual investors as well as local and state governments began to buy. A tidal wave of cash flowed through the economy, and, after the momentary setback of 911, the stock market recovered to reach the levels it had achieved in the late 90s. The trap was set.

Now the very banksters who had conned the public into buying their products started smearing derivatives while cutting off the supply of unlimited fiat cash. The sub-prime market was the first to implode and in a single day the DOW fell 777 points. This is the context in which the infamous Banker Bailouts and the Stimulus Bill were passed.

The very banksters who had caused the crisis through a strategy of fraud then held the congress hostage and basically said write us a blank check or the economy dies—and by the way there will be Martial Law in America (several Congress-men said they actually received such threats). Although Congress put up a fight, eventually they capitulated and when all was said and done, $23.7 trillion was created as a line of credit as billions of tax payer dollars went offshore to *European* Banks. This abominable heist was the biggest transfer of wealth and the biggest scam in history. These greedy, insol-vent zombiebanks destroyed and devastated our economy (in the name of a post-industrial society) and then got bailed out because they were too big to fail. But recall, that's *exactly* how the Fed was designed to work all along. This wasn't an accident. This was by design.

With their blank check (essentially), the banksters have been consolidating their empire as they mop up that which remains of the middle class. The debt we allegedly owe them (if you count their fraudulent derivatives) is between 20 and 100 times the *Global* GDP. This might as well be infinite debt because it is mathematically impossible to pay back. As a pundit recently said on CNBC, we are all just slaves working for banksters and their world government—which already exists in a limited and informal way. I truly believe that the global elites are now getting all of their ducks in a row. Once all has been consolidated and mopped up to their satisfaction, the final implosion will occur. When it does occur and the dollar dies, trillions in offshore holdings will come flooding back into our market from China, Japan, Saudi Arabia, and Europe, creating massive hyperinflation. There will be civil unrest like we've never seen before and the DHS police state will drop the hammer. FEMA camps will go live and I believe there is a risk of civil war (which would make us vulnerable to foreign invasion). This economic take-down is the ultimate False Flag!

In the next chapter, we'll follow yet another thread from the 19th century to the present time. This thread will help to explain why the New World Order is so utterly ruthless and vicious!

But now it's time to update *The Omega Manifesto*.

27) The same powers behind the Fed set up the CFR which is the establishment / shadow government in America. These same people created the United Nations, the Bilderberg Group, and the Trilateral Commission, which are all working in tandem to move us towards World Government.

28) While establishing structures that will lead to global economic and political integration, the NWO has engaged in a subversive cultural revolution using education and the media to re-program the public.

29) The False Flag is a go-to play in the globalist playbook.

30) A coming financial storm (of which 2008 was only an appetizer) will be the mother of all false flags and will signal the final take down of America and the West and emergence of a truly global government.

Chapter 7 Endnotes

(1) Gary Kah, *En Route to Global Occupation*, 36.
(2) Ibid.
(3) Dr. John Coleman, *Conspirators' Hierarchy,* 2007.
(4) Kah, *En Route*, 39.
(5) Dr. Dennis Cuddy, *The Power Elite and the Secret Nazi Plan*, 24-25.
(6) http://en.wikiquote.org/wiki/David_Rockefeller
(7) They Sold Their Souls for Rock n' Roll
(8) Ibid.
(9) Dennis Cuddy, "The Power Elite's Historical Outline Part 4"— Newswithviews url accessed July 31, 2012
(10) Ibid.
(11) Ibid.
(12) Ibid.
(13) John Loeffler, Worldview Wars, (Steel on Steel Productions, 2010-2011).
(14) Ibid.
(15) Ibid.
(16) Paul Smith, *New Evangelicalism: New World Order*, 21.
(17) *Endgame,* Alex Jones Productions, 2007.
(18) *Terrorstorm,* Alex Jones Productions, 2007.
       Cuddy, *Nazi Plan*, 56.

See also the Alex Jones Films, *The Obama Deception* and *Fall of the Republic*.

Chapter 8—Eugenics, the Environment, and Beyond

Few people are aware of just how influential the eugenics movement was in the early part of the 20th century. Even fewer are aware that eugenics continues to have a great influence on several key scientific disciplines to this day, including environmentalism. This chapter will follow an undeniable thread that neatly ties together the genesis of a pseudo-scientific movement (eugenics) and the alarming and little-known endgame of that movement's philosophical and scientific progeny today in the 21st century.

The foundation of eugenics was initially laid by Thomas Malthus (1766-1834) at the end of the 18th century (though it is worth noting that Plato's *Republic* describes a hypothetical system of selective breeding). Malthus promoted the idea that charity was immoral because it perpetuated generational poverty, an idea Malthus claimed "simply made no sense in the natural scheme of human progress."[1] This Malthusian doctrine served as a forerunner to Social Darwinism, which is "the notion that in the struggle to survive in a harsh world, many humans [are] not only less worthy, many [are] actually destined to wither away as a rite of progress."[2] To Social Darwinists, preserving the weak and needy is an unnatural act."[3] Francis Galton (1822-1911), the father of eugenics and Biometrics[4] and the half cousin of Charles Darwin, viewed the weak and the needy as genetically unfit and advocated eliminating them via "segregation, deportation, castration, marriage prohibition, compulsory sterilization, passive euthanasia—and ultimately extermination."(5) Galton believed that the "worst elements" of society should be discouraged from breeding while the elite, of course, should be encouraged to freely reproduce. But think about it. The methodologies and mechanisms for determining just who should be categorized as "weak and needy" are highly subjective. Plus the potential for those making such a determination to abuse their authority in the pursuit of power is astronomical. Eugenics, one could easily argue, had pseudo-science written all over it from the very beginning. Predictably, opportunistic elites saw eugenics "as a means of developing the 'social control' they desired"(6) and the funding quickly began to pour in. In 1890, funded by the Carnegie Institute and the Rockefeller and Harriman families, the Cold Spring Harbor Laboratory began conducting genetic research experiments—headed by Daniel Coit Gilman of Skull and Bones.(7)

By 1907, the first sterilization laws were on the books in the United States, specifically in the State of Indiana.(8) In 1911 the Rockefellers began funding the Kaiser Wilhelm Institute in Germany which would later serve as the scientific brainchild of the Nazis and the Third Reich.(9) By 1927, twenty-seven US States had passed sterilization laws(10) and by the mid 1930s that number had grown to 34.(11) Incredibly, these laws stayed on the books until as late as the 1970s(12) and at least 60,000 Americans were sterilized during this time period as a part of the eugenics movement.(13)

In April of 1933, Nazi Ernst Rudin of the aforementioned Kaiser Wilhelm Institute wrote an article for Margaret Sanger's *Birth Control Review* entitled "Eugenic Sterilization: An Urgent Need."(14) Margaret Sanger, founder of Planned

Parenthood and H. G. Wells' lover, taught that Jews, Gypsies, and Blacks possessed "dysgenic stock" while Rudin taught a young Josef Mengele, the Nazi Angel of Death who was one of the most wicked individuals who ever lived.(15) The Nazis exterminated six million Jews as the logical conclusion of Social Darwinism and eugenics. The occultist elites of the Third Reich believed themselves to be the descendents of a super Aryan race and that they were helping to move the evolutionary process forward through their extermination program. Disturbingly, the same elites who funded the eugenicist pseudo-scientists throughout the early part of the 20th century also aided the Nazi war effort in the 30s and 40s—largely through corporations under their control. Here are just a few examples: The DuPont chemical company advocated "the injection of special drugs to create a race of supermen."(16) General Motors produced trucks, armored cars, and tanks in Germany all throughout the 1930s.(17) The Ford Motor Company, as late as 1940 "refused to build aircraft engines for England and instead built supplies of the five-ton military trucks that were the backbone of German army transportation."(18) Rockefeller Standard Oil provided the enemy fuel by way of neutral Switzerland(19) while Chase Bank in Nazi-occupied Paris continued to do millions in business with Germany well-after Pearl Harbor.(20) IBM provided the punch card technology (literally eugenics machines) that the Nazis used to identify and catalog Jews during World War II.(21)

By the end of World War II, the war criminals of the Third Reich had unwittingly discredited eugenics (the pseudo-science the Nazis had simply imported from America and England) and, following World War II, the movement had to re-brand its image. Galton's blatant rhetoric, with the aid of propaganda techniques pioneered by Edward Bernays (nephew of Sigmund Freud), had to be toned-down and re-packaged. The eugenicists therefore began re-framing their agenda in terms of population growth and over-population.(22) This terminology gave rise to the new scientific fields of population control, genetics, and environmentalism.(23) But notice, these new 'scientific" disciplines were established on the philosophical foundation of a pseudo-science—eugenics.

In 1945 the United Nations was established, representing a major step towards a "World Superstate."(24) In 1946, Sir Julian Huxely, the first Director-General of UNESCO, wrote a paper entitled "UNESCO: Its Purpose and its Philosophy" in which he stated that the goal of UNESCO was "to help the emergence of a single world culture."(25) Huxley, whose family was involved in a failed inbreeding program involving the Darwins and the Galtons, further wrote that for "the first time in history . . . the mechanisms for world unification have become available."(26) Huxley continues in the document:

> "Thus even though it is quite true that any radical eugenic policy will be for many years politically and psychologically impossible, it will be important for UNESCO to see that the eugenic problem is examined with the greatest care, and that the public mind is informed of the issues at stake so that much that now is unthinkable may at least become thinkable. . . ."(27)

The document goes on to describe UNESCO's task as that of social control / social engineering and implies the inevitability of "a technological intellectual elite."(28) It should be apparent by now that the United Nations, UNESCO, and the world's elite desire a global scientific dictatorship. Bertrand Russell, one of the leading intellectuals of his generation, gloated that "the whole development of scientific technique has made it easier than it used to be to maintain a despotic rule of a minority."(29) In a 1962 speech at UC Berkeley shortly before his death, Aldous Huxley, brother of UNESCO's Sir Julian Huxley and author of "Brave New World" stated:

> "If you are going to control any population for any length of time, you must have some measure of consent . . . sooner or later you have to bring in an element of persuasion, an element of getting people to consent to what is happening to them."(30)

So how do technocrats and social engineers achieve such control? As we have seen, two of the greatest weapons in their arsenal are control of mass media (using Bernaysian propaganda techniques) and control of the education system (John Dewey's humanistic psycho-social indoctrination centers aka public schools). For half a century, the public, from a very early age, has been subjected to a brutal regiment of propaganda and indoctrination techniques that basically amount to brainwashing and mind control.

In 1961 UNESCO's Sir Julian Huxley, President of the British Eugenics Society, founded the World Wildlife Fund.(31) Prince Bernard of the Netherlands, former SS officer in Nazi Germany and co-founder of the Bilderberg Group, was the WWF's first President.(32) The WWF, bankrolled once again by ubiquitous Rockefeller dollars, is a high level New World Order front organization that at one time was headed by Prince Philip (1981-1996).(33) His Royal Highness, of course, has stated that he wishes to be reincarnated as a killer virus to 'cull' surplus human populations.

The UN and organizations like the World Wildlife Fund masquerade as humanitarian entities with a moral obligation to eradicate poverty and save the environment—cunningly framing the "population" issue as an environmental issue. Yet, because there exists a positive correlation between population growth, economic growth, and industrialization in developing nations, the UN finds population control measures far preferable to promoting genuine economic development in the Third World and Africa.(34) This important concept sheds light on the fact that the UN, as a matter of institutional policy, champions a worldwide zero-growth, post-industrial society. When one cuts through the propaganda, the planetary utopia the UN envisions for the future is nothing more than a neo-feudalistic system with technocratic overlords regulating every aspect of human existence—the majority of humanity becoming servile serfs.

Frank Notestein, President of John D. Rockefeller's Population Council (six of the Council's ten founding members were eugenicists) admitted in a 1969 paper that "to achieve zero rate of population growth governments will have to do more than cajole; they will have to coerce."(35) Notestein, also a member of the American Eugenics Society, the Council on Foreign Relations, and the first Director of the UN Population Division, likewise conceded that "the price for this type of population control may well be the institution of a totalitarian regime."(36)

In that same year (1969), Robert McNamara, at the time the fifth President of the World Bank (which provides loans to developing nations) stated that he was hesitant to fund health care in the Third World "unless it was very strictly related to population control, because usually health facilities contributed to the decline of the death rate, and thereby to the population explosion."(37) (McNamara had previously served as President of the Ford Motor Company and went on to become the Secretary of Defense under Presidents Kennedy and Johnson.)

The stated goal of the World Bank is the reduction of Third World poverty. But, by controlling the money that developing nations will or won't receive, those nations end up becoming dependent on the World Bank, their sovereignty is undermined, and in most cases, development is actually mitigated. Similarly, the International Monetary Fund uses foreign aid as a weapon to control natural resources.(38) However, due to indoctrination and brainwashing techniques employed by the mass media and public schools, the vast majority of the public (if they even know what the World Bank and IMF are in the first place) has no idea that these two institutions, instead of promoting self-sufficiency and eradicating poverty, are actually promoting poverty and subjugation in the Third World. How many humanitarians, whose hearts are in the right place, would be horrified to discover that the UN, the World Bank, and the IMF are actually agents of the very imperialism activists consistently decry? Ironically, these activists are unwittingly promoting a new form of neo-imperialism under the banner of humanitarianism. The "idea of developing nations taking charge of their destiny [is] anathema"(39) to control-freak technocratic dictators who feed at the trough of offshore megabanks. The point is, elites don't care so much about the environment as they care about controlling people (if they are lucky enough to be allowed to live).

Recall Aldous Huxley's observation that population control would require a certain level of consent on the part of the masses. The brutality and horror of sterilization, abortion, one-child policies, euthanasia, and infanticide would only carry the eugenics agenda so far. It is worth repeating that the 'science' of population control is a means of controlling populations and engineering societies through various scientific techniques. High level Rockefeller globalist Zbigniew Brzezinski wrote of such techniques in 1970:

> "Such a society would be dominated by an elite whose claim to power would rest on allegedly superior scientific know-how. . . . This elite would not hesitate to achieve its political ends by using the latest modern techniques for influencing public behavior and keeping society under close surveillance and control."(40)

Brzezinski, who served as National Security Advisor to Jimmy Carter and more recently advised the Obama administration, elaborates in his book *The Technotronic Era* (which was commissioned by the Club of Rome)(41):

> "At the same time the capacity to assert social and political control over the individual will vastly increase. It will soon be possible to assert almost continuous control over every citizen and to maintain up-to-date files, containing even the most personal details about health and personal behavior of every citizen in addition to the more customary data.

> "These files will be subject to instantaneous retrieval by the authorities. Power will gravitate into

the hands of those who control information. Our existing institutions will be supplanted by pre-crisis management institutions, the task of which will be to identify in advance likely social crises and to develop programs to cope with them. [To this end, Google, a front for the National Security Agency on record, has developed algorithms which project future trends with great accuracy.]

"This will encourage tendencies through the next several decades toward a technotronic era, a dictatorship, leaving even less room for political procedures as we know them. Finally, looking ahead to the end of the century, the possibility of biochemical mind control and genetic tinkering with man, including beings which will function like men and reason like them as well, could give rise to some difficult questions. [This will be addressed in chapter ten.]"(42)

Brzezinski's book was projecting out into the future (remember it was written in 1970). During the intervening period some of the old "crass" techniques of population control (sterilization, abortion, euthanasia et al.) continued to be employed. Technology had to catch up to Brzezinski's dystopic vision (as it now has).

As an example of the old methodolgies, Henry Kissinger's infamous 1974 National Security Study Memorandum (NSSM 200) essentially made eugenics official US foreign policy, with devastating effects. The memorandum builds on the premise that if Third World Nations were allowed to develop too quickly, the resulting population increase would cause "a major risk of severe damage to world economic, political, and ecological systems."(43) With breath-taking irony, the white paper actually states that such damage to existing structures and the ensuing chaos it would create would inevitably cause damage "to our humanitarian values."(44)

Such is the New World Order. They call evil good and good evil. Their warped logic would be humorous if the results weren't so deadly. NSSM 200 then called for the US, the UN, and other international bodies to implement zero-growth policies world wide, with particular emphasis on "India, Bangladesh, Pakistan, Nigeria, Mexico, Indonesia, Brazil, the Philippines, Thailand, Egypt, Turkey, Ethiopia, and Colombia."(45) Kissinger proposes "increased assistance for family planning services" and creating "conditions conducive to fertility decline" as two ways of bringing about zero-growth. The result?

1) By 1976 six million men and two million women in India had been sterilized.(46)

2) An official government investigation revealed that during the same time period "an estimated 44% of all Brazilian women aged between 14 and 55 had been permanently sterilized."(47)

3) By 1978 China's infamous one child policy began to emerge, greatly assisted (of course) by the International Planned Parenthood Federation and the UN Population Fund.(48) Participation was initially voluntary, but by 1983 "coercion became official Chinese policy."(49)

Anybody who hasn't been sleeping under a rock knows at least some of the horror that followed in China. Forced abortions, forced sterilizations, and infanticide became commonplace. The Communist Chinese created custom execution vans to satisfy the emergence of a black market where freshly harvested body parts and organs of "euthanasia" victims were sold to the highest bidder. Unbelievably, not only did the UN turn a blind eye to this demonic brutality, it actually gave Population Awards to Xinzhong Qian and Indira Gandhi to "reward their accomplishments in limiting population growth in China and India."(50) Of course, all of this still goes on. Yet when one considers that the "science" of population control was built upon the foundation of eugenics and endorsed by known eugenicists, such wicked fruit begins to make much more sense. In a humanistic, Darwinistic, collectivist world, people exist for the State, which is seen as god. Those who don't serve any purpose for the state are disposable dead weight.

Environmentalism

As already stated, the globalist eugenics cult frames the population control issue as an environmental issue. Thus a direct link between eugenics and environmentalism has already been established. Confirming this connection, environmentalist and futurist James Lovelock, in a 2008 interview, told *The London Guardian* that:

> "Those who fail to see that population growth and climate change are two sides of the same coin are either ignorant or hiding from the truth. These two huge environmental problems are inseparable and to discuss one while ignoring the other is irrational."(51)

[Note: Lovelock has recently recanted some of his views and has come out against environmental alarmism.]

Furthermore, many "of the revered forerunners of the modern environmentalists favored eugenics programs aimed at reshaping the human race according to their own standards of perfection."(52) One such revered forerunner was Harrison Brown. Known as "a key philosophical guru"(53) of the modern green movement, Brown was quite openly a eugenicist. In his book *The Challenge of Man's Future* (1954), Brown pontificated:

> "Thus we could sterilize or in other ways discourage the mating of the feeble-minded. We could go further and systematically attempt to prune from society, by prohibiting them from breeding, persons suffering from serious inheritable forms of physical defects, such as congenital deafness, dumbness, blindness, or absence of limbs."(54)

Note again the Darwinian presuppositions of elites like Brown, who are essentially saying, "We are in charge of God's selection process for planet Earth."(55) One of Brown's great admirers in recent times has been President Obama's Science Czar John Holdren. In a 1986 essay, Holdren lauded Brown, writing:

> "Thirty years after Harrison Brown elaborated these positions, it remains difficult to improve on them as a coherent depiction of the perils and challenges we face. . . . It is a book, in short, that should have reshaped permanently the perceptions of all serious analysts."(56)

Holdren has in in his writings over the years advocated compulsory population control laws, forced abortions, mass sterilization through drugs in drinking water, all to be enforced by a planetary regime and an armed international police force.(57)

The logical conclusion of this Eugenic Social Darwinism is a scientific dictatorship. There is no other way it can go. Under the auspices of the United Nations, Green Techno-Fascists like Obama administration Science Czar John Holdren are aiming at a *global* scientific dictatorship. And they are not above using junk science to hit their mark. Think about it. If the eugenics movement of the early part of the 20th century was so demonstrably a pseudo-science, and if eugenics is demonstrably the forerunner of the modern day environmental movement, is it so surprising that the Green Movement is under-girded by half-baked pop-science and blatant propaganda? "Junk science requires more junk science to perpetuate itself."(58) So when Al Gore boldly announces, despite clear evidence to the contrary, that the global scientific community has reached consensus regarding climate change, it shouldn't come as any surprise. He is merely manifesting the spirit of his movement—there is consensus because I, the great green techno-fascist goblin, say there is consensus. Never mind the following hypocrisies.

Al Gore owns more than $500,000 worth in shares of Occidental Petroleum and helped to set up a no bid contract for Occidental to purchase the US Naval Oil Reserve.(59) (Meanwhile Greens who follow Gore demonize big oil and push to ban drilling.) Along the same lines, the World Wildlife Fund was funded and run by Royal Dutch Shell from the very beginning, a fact which helps to expose that organizations duplicitous objectives.(60) Prince Charles, son of the great enviro-hero Prince Philip, "owns a million acres of forested land in Wales from which timber is regularly harvested.(61) We also know that "some of the largest companies, allegedly 'polluting' the earth, are the largest contributors of funds to the environmental movement."(62) Many readers will also recall that in the 1970's the Greens where prophesying a global ice age, before switching over to the global warming narrative, and later global climate change. Now John Holdren says it's global climate "disruption." James Heiser's analysis is right on:

> "The nebulousness of such terminology would allow Holdren's fellow extremists to simply attribute *any* unusual meteorological event to the insidious forces of 'global climate disruption.' Thus 'global climate disruption' becomes 'The Theory Which Explains Everything'—and is therefore utterly worthless (at least scientifically), because it is unfalsifiable, and therefore unscientific."(63)

Scientists who go against the grain of climate alarmism are systematically marginalized and, if necessary demonized. Those who refuse to tow the green line are denied government grants, positions at universities, and funding from the Rockefeller and Ford Foundations.(64) As the fallout from climategate demonstrated, there is an ever-widening gap between public opinion and the alleged scientific consensus. Yet the radical environmentalists view the public as dumbed-down serfs destined to be dominated in their imminent neo-feudalistic global scientific dictatorship.

Agenda 21

As already stated, the technocratic elite do not care so much about saving the environment or ending Third World poverty as they care about controlling people. The endgame of their eugenic, population control agenda largely manifests in the form of Agenda 21. Working in tandem with the Convention on Biodiversity, Agenda 21 came out of the 1992 Rio Earth Summit (UNCED), held in Rio de Janeiro, Brazil. The Rio Earth Summit represents a watershed moment in the history of the environmental movement. Gary Kah explains:

> "The Convention on Biodiversity created the framework for nations to develop strategies and make international commitments for conserving biological diversity. Though this sounds benign, the implementation of this treaty [has allowed] international groups and national government agencies to elevate environmental protection to draconian levels. Agenda 21, on the other hand, has been expanded to contain everything needed to internationally regulate life—from agriculture to transportation, from our children to reproductive rights."(65)

Gary rightly points out that "the Rio Earth Summit provided a great boost to the global government movement."(66) It is precisely because environmental issues are perceived as transcending national boundaries that the Green movement was hand-picked as a means of strengthening international cooperation and global organizing. At a nuts and bolts level, this cooperation often occurs by working through non-governmental organizations (NGOs). A document released by the

International Institute for Sustainable Development (IISD) corroborates this conclusion:

> "These efforts at the global level directly contributed to building a sense of global identity, or global citizenship which would be the first step towards global governance. Such global governance would further distance power from the people while giving unlimited access to governments and multinationals."(67)

Where eugenics built upon the foundation of Social Darwinism, the modern Green Movement presupposes a communitarian worldview that is hostile to both free markets, private property, and individual liberties. While Agenda 21 was never ratified in the United States, it has nevertheless been systematically implemented at the national, state, and local levels in the period following UNCED.(68)

Does this sound familiar? People show up from out of town—often in more rural areas—talking about Smart Growth or some other environmental cause. The new arrivals may say that your town "has been chosen" for the particular project, which of course plays on pride in one's community. Soon the new folks in town are conducting meetings in which "facilitators" are skillfully engineering a false consensus (based on the Dialectical process), moving people towards a pre-determined outcome while creating the illusion of democratic process. Before people realize what is happening, one has to jump through ridiculous bureaucratic hoops, paying exorbitant taxes and fees to perform even the simplest of tasks—like changing one's roof tiles. When all is said and done, folks are forced to sell their property and move "into town," where regulations and taxes are more manageable. Their property is now "green" and Agenda 21 has worked like a charm! This is manipulation and social engineering at its very worst because in general people can't put their finger on what is wrong until it is already too late.

The migration of people out of rural areas into more urban areas is no coincidence. The non-redacted version of the Convention on Biodiversity (that came out of UNCED) literally calls for populations to be moved into highly controlled compact cities where travel into unauthorized zones is restricted.(69) This corresponds neatly with the aims of the Wildlands Network (formerly the Wildlands Project), an NGO which exists to create protected zones in North America, ostensibly to rescue animal species facing extinction. According to the Convention, these cities, or population centers, are to be connected via superhighways—like the NAFTA Superhighway, which elites are attempting to build in conjunction with the emerging North American Union, as we have seen. Disturbingly, exits to rural areas along certain stretches of highway are already being walled off to prevent an invasive humanity from entering protected Green Zones.(70) To this end, Yale University professor Karen Seto told MSNBC:

> "We certainly don't want (humans) strolling about the entire countryside. We want them to save land for nature by living closely [together]."(71)

If global elites only wanted to move humanity into these compact prison cities, it would be bad enough—indeed, worthy of a new revolution. But the Green Techno-Fascists don't stop there. The current world population is seven billion. If elites have their way, the global population will be reduced to

2 billion, 1 billion, or even 500 million—depending on whom you ask. Put another way, between 71 and 93 percent of the world's "useless eaters"—that's between 5 and 6.5 *billion*—should be liquidated. Among those who openly support this view are Prince Philip, Ted Turner (who also advocates a "voluntary" global one child policy)(72), and Bill Gates of Microsoft and Monsanto.

Sound over the top? A biography on Julian Huxley that appears on the Galton Institute website (formerly the British Eugenics Society) states that Huxley believed "a catastrophic event may be needed for evolution to move at an accelerated pace."(73) Dr. Eric R. Pianka, a biologist at the University of Texas (Austin) has an idea for causing such a catastrophe. An airborne Ebola virus, Pianka says, could be introduced that would "exterminate 90% of the world's population."(74) While Pianka may sound like a fringe lunatic, it is disturbing to know how closely Pianka's outlook aligns with Green Technocratic Elites who seek to implement their global scientific dictatorship sooner rather than later.

Population Reduction

And in case the reader is inclined to think this can't happen, or even that God won't allow it to happen, consider the following. Revelation 6:8 states that in the last days, 25% of the world population will be killed via war, disease, famine, and wild animals. Based upon a current world population of 7 billion, that means 1.75 billion will be killed. Revelation 9:18 further states that an additional third of the world population will be destroyed through plagues introduced by demonic hoards. Based upon the figure 5.25 (7—1.75), that means *another* 1.75 billion will die. This means that almost exactly 50% of the global population will be killed in the time just preceding Christ's return, and this figure may not include deaths caused by the collateral damage resulting from the other judgments. Jesus Himself said that if those days were not shortened no flesh would be saved (Matthew 24:22).

The alarming figure almost certainly does not include those who will be martyred for their faith in Christ during this period. As the next chapter will show, we are rapidly approaching a time when true Christianity will be separated from false, apostate Christianity. False Christianity will not be able to stand in the face of what is coming down the pike.

As a matter of fact, if we are honest, we must admit that the soft-kill agenda is already underway. We know there are cancer viruses and heavy metals in vaccines, fluoride and radioactive isotopes in the water, strontium and barium salts in the chemtrails, GMO crops and high fructose corn syrup in the food, and we know that nuclear reactors are belching out hot particles into the atmosphere all throughout the Northern Hemisphere. In the name of population control and saving the environment we are all being incrementally murdered!

Though this chapter has revealed only the tip of the iceberg, it has conclusively shown that the pseudo-sciences of eugenics, population control, and environmentalism are working in conjunction to form a "global transnational movement" that seeks "to reduce world population through global governance."(75) And with that said, let us add to *The Omega Manifesto*:

31) The crack-pot science of modern day radical environmentalism is the present manifestation of the crack-pot science of eugenics.

32) If global elites have their way, the world population will be reduced from 7 billion to somewhere between 500 million and 2 billion.

Chapter 8 Endnotes

(1) Marshall, Andrew Gavin. "The New Eugenics and the Rise of the Global Scientific Dictatorship: The Technological Revolution and the Future of Freedom, Part 3." Global Research, July 5, 2010.
(2) Ibid.
(3) Ibid.
(4) Galton.org mainpage, accessed April 17, 2012.
(5) Marshall, "The New Eugenics."
(6) Cuddy, Dr. Dennis L. "The Power Elite and the Secret Nazi Plan." (Oklahoma City: Bible Belt Publishing, 2011), 95.
(7) Ibid., 95-96. / Endgame: Blueprint for Global Enslavement (Jones Productions, 2007).
(8) Endgame, 2007.Taylor, Daniel. "Eugenics and Environmentalism: From quality control to quantity control." (Old-Thinker News, April 30, 2008).
(9) Cuddy, "Secret Nazi Plan", 33. / Endgame, 2007.
(10) Endgame, 2007.
(11) Taylor, "Eugenics and Environmentalism".
(12) Ibid.
(13) Marshall, "The New Eugenics."
(14) Cuddy, "Secret Nazi Plan," 33.
(15) Ibid.
(16) Ibid., 93.
(17) Ibid.
(18) Ibid., 93-94.
(19) Ibid., 94.
(20) Ibid., 10-11.
(21) Ibid., 11-12.
(22) Taylor, "Eugenics and Environmentalism."
(23) Marshall, "The New Eugenics."
(24) Allen, Gary. "None Dare Call It a Conspiracy." (Rossmoor, California: Concord Press, 1971), 86.
(25) Marshall, "The New Eugenics."
(26) Ibid.
(27) Ibid.
(28) Ibid.
(29) Ibid.
(30) Ibid.
(31) Ibid.

(32) Ibid.
(33) Coleman, Dr. John. "Conspirators' Hierarchy: The Story of the Committee of 300." (Bozeman, MT: American Publishers, 1992), 52.
(34) Marshall, "The New Eugenics."
(35) Taylor, "Eugenics and Environmentalism."
(36) Ibid.
(37) Marshall, "The New Eugenics."
(38) Coleman, "Committee of 300," 11.
(39) Ibid.
(40) Marshall, "The New Eugenics."
(41) Coleman, "Committee of 300," 27.
(42) Ibid., 28.
(43) Marshall, "The New Eugenics."
(44) Ibid.
(45) Ibid.
(46) Ibid.
(47) Ibid.
(48) Ibid.
(49) Ibid.
(50) Ibid.
(51) Ibid.
(52) Heiser, James. "The Link Between Eugenics & Global Warming Hype." (The New American, April 5, 2011.)
(53) Ibid.
(54) Ibid.
(55) Kah, Gary H. "The New World Religion." (Noblesville, Indiana: Hope International Publishing, Inc., 1999), 119.
(56) Heiser, "Eugenics & Global Warming Hype."
(57) http://zombietime.com/john_holdren/—accessed 04/20/2012
(58) Heiser, "Eugenics & Global Warming Hype."
(59) Hennington, Patrick. "Big Green Oil Money: WWF founded and run by Royal Dutch-Shell." (Infowars.com, April 13, 2012).—accessed 04/13/2012
(60) Ibid.
(61) Coleman, "Committee of 300", 139.
(62) Ibid.
(63) Heiser, "Eugenics & Global Warming Hype."
(64) Ibid.
(65) Kah, "The New World Religion," 145-146.

(66) Ibid., 146.
(67) Ibid.
(68) Steel on Steel radio broadcast, 07/31/2010—"Agenda 21 Plus 20."
(69) Endgame, 2007.
(70) Ibid.
(71) Watson, Paul Joseph. "Green Fascism: The Growing Threat of Eco-Tyranny." (Infowars.com, accessed 04/09/2012).
(72) Taylor, "Eugenics and Environmentalism."
(73) Marshall, "The New Eugenics."
(74) Watson, "Green Fascism."
(75) Marshall, "The New Eugenics."

Chapter 9—The Church and the New World Order

Chapter 10 is the payoff chapter. We'll look at the coming New World Order in light of everything we have already seen. But we have one last loose end that we need to tie up before we can get into that. Much of the philosophical and academic content of this book may seem disconnected from church life. I would argue that if this is the case, it is because our churches have failed us. To quote John Loeffler one more time, much of the non-directive Bible babble we hear preached on Sundays is completely disconnected from our lives the other six days of the week. We have been content to draw our circles and to reside safely and comfortably within a protective bubble while we play church and mindlessly spout Christian clichés and pseudo-spiritual platitudes. We have been threatened by the intellectuals of the world and we have been unwilling to engage them in a substantive way. But if Christianity is *really* true, then it is *we* who possess the truth, not they. Not that other systems of the world contain no truth, but they do not contain the whole truth. Yet I have been encouraged by the small, but formidable remnant within the Church which has not been content to remain on the defensive cowering in fear, but who have taken to the offensive, attacking the false philosophical systems of the world at a foundational level—which is precisely what this book has endeavored to do.

While some in the church have mistakenly retreated to the safety of their church bubbles, countless others have made the opposite mistake of accommodating the spirit of the age. In short, they try to reach the world by becoming the world. It is this group that is the focus of this chapter. What follows is an essay I wrote that appeared in the Fall 2011 edition of the Hope for the World Update, the quarterly newsletter published by Gary Kah. (There are a couple of insignificant changes that I made for this book.)

An Unavoidable Question

You can answer the question now or you can answer the question later. But sooner or later you are going to have to answer the question. There is a great wave towering over Evangelicals like a tsunami, and when the wave crashes there will be no more time for procrastination. One way or another, we will all take our stand. But will we stand with the worldly, politically correct, apostate church, or will we stand with the Biblical, called-out, Body of Christ? The German church once procrastinated. The German church once attempted to ride out the wave. The German church once compromised.

J. Vernon McGee famously warned that one day the true church in America would be forced to go underground, noting that it would be the mainline denominations leading the charge in the marginalization of God's people. Presently John Loeffler warns of a great flying wedge rushing headlong towards Evangelicals.(1) (Wedges divide.) In his book *The Great Evangelical Disaster*, Francis Schaeffer identified the watershed issue that will separate the true Church from the apostate church.

While I don't claim to see the whole picture perfectly, I believe I can identify where the wave is coming from. Even more fundamentally, I believe I can identify the wave. The wave is the apostate church, a wolf in sheep's clothing that preaches a watery gospel, which is no gospel at all. This church teaches a man-centered self-help message to itching, self-absorbed ears. On the authority of God's Word, an apostate church is rising, a great falling away is coming, and the dawn of a new spiritual world order is upon us. Persecution is coming to true Christians in America and the West.

The Book of Revelation describes a complete global system under the authority of an autocratic dictator. The Apocalypse of Jesus Christ clearly paints a picture of a worldwide empire that rests upon three legs—an economic leg, a political leg, and a spiritual leg. Conservative Evangelical scholars and prophecy teachers have often tended to focus on the economic and political legs, yet Revelation makes it clear that the spiritual leg *is in control* of the other two. The woman rides the beast. The false prophet has power over the global economic system. The scenario described is a bit enigmatic at first glance.

The political and economic mechanisms and institutions of the coming New World Order are rapidly moving into position. Yet I have always wondered, how do you go about creating a new world religion? Furthermore, how will that religion gain control of a worldwide political and economic system? I have never been satisfied by those who simply say it's going to be the Roman Catholic Church that pulls it off, or the other camp that says it's going to be an Islamic caliphate. (I believe that both sides offer valuable prophetic insights.) But now, though I certainly don't claim to have all of the answers, I believe that I am on the right track, at least in terms of the methodology being used to bring about this global transformational spirituality.

Let us first examine the political and economic legs very briefly. Doing so will make it easier for us to understand the methodologies that are being utilized to organize the emerging religious leg.

The Political and Economic Legs

You can hide your head in the sand if you want to, but key figures in politics, economics, and the media are openly talking about a New World Order and global governance. Ten years ago you could get away with calling someone a conspiracy theorist for bringing up this subject, but now the agenda is being discussed and pursued so openly that the security blanket accusation of conspiracy theory has lost its effectiveness. You are free to insist upon utilizing this tactic, of course, but in doing so you are only betraying your own ignorance. Because of the out in the open nature of the agenda, the emergence of a new political and economic paradigm is not difficult for researchers to track. I have been doing it for almost a decade.

It is fairly evident to me that the governance of the New World Order will be the fruit of Fabian socialism with fascist characteristics. In short, big government in bed with big business, a synthesis of crony capitalism and state socialism. For elites, the police state control grid tyranny of socialism is ideal. But socialism has repeatedly failed economically. And everybody knows it (except the leftist talking heads who get on TV and play dumb to dupe the masses). Enter corrupt Wall Street business interests, who enjoy cartel status (shared monopolies), illegal tax exemptions, and regulatory immunity. (Even the great leftist messiah Obama filled his cabinet with these people!) But why does this go on? It's pretty simple really. In exchange for providing the economic engine that will be necessary to keep the Marxist game going in the future global state (Keynesian interventions), the government provides the big boys with insider deals while simultaneously regulating the little guy out of business (tax the snot out of 'em and give 'em mountains of red tape). Folks, this is fascism!

Mikhail Gorbachev openly talked about this, a synthesis of the United States and the USSR. The United States has become a socialist nation by evolution, not by revolution. The radicals of the 60s took a bath, got a haircut, and infiltrated the culture at key points of power. They have used our own liberties and institutions against us and now the United States has become a nation the older generation doesn't even recognize. How were these radicals able to achieve such great success in so short a time? Through the dialectical methodology [we looked at in chapter one).

The Dia-what?

Traditional western intellectuals operated on a philosophical foundation that assumed there were absolutes in the universe such as Natural Law. In other words, it is perfectly rational to say murder is wrong because there is such a thing as right and wrong. There are absolute truths in the universe. In the past, if somebody came along and tried to sell you on the idea that murder is right, their thesis could immediately be rejected, like so:

A is not equal to non-A (B), the first rule of classical logic.

A is true (Murder is wrong). B is not true (Murder is acceptable). Traditional Westerners picked A every time.

— 168 —

But in our time this philosophical assumption has been rejected and a new system of logic has resulted. I won't trace the the whole history of it here (I recommend the Francis Schaeffer *Trilogy* if you are interested in the subject), but modern man—particularly the power elite—has come up with a new philosophy based upon the rejection of the notion of absolute truth. So if you come along and tell me murder is right, that is a valid truth claim in the brave new world. Through dialogue, we can come to a new synthesis where both A and non-A contributed in the outcome. You have your truth, I have mine.

> A is valid (Murder is wrong). B is valid (Murder is acceptable). Dialogue.
> C is the synthesis that comes out of our discussion. (Murder is acceptable on Tuesday at 10 a.m. if the watermelon is ripe).

This is the methodology of the New World Order. The power elite play A against B as if they are enemies or rivals (like Democrats and Republicans), but C is the outcome the power elite had in mind all along (the syntheseis, USA and USSR). The contentious bickering between A and B is largely for public consumption so that citizens feel like they are involved in and contributing to the political process. The whole idea is to move society from traditional values (Judea-Christian values), to transitional values (compromised), to transformational values (progressive globalist approved amoral double-think). Another way of describing this three-step process: Problem (never let a good crisis go to waste), reaction (we need change), solution (desired outcome, forward).

This methodology is used, almost monolithically, in economics, educational curricula, social engineering, government, and corporate management. What's more, since the 1980s, the Dialectical process has been used to compromise the church. This manipulative and corrupt technique, based upon the philosophical foundation of moral relativism, has been introduced into the Body of Christ. To make matters worse, many pastors are lauding it. Some of the pastors are simply naïve. Others, I believe, are complicit.

I am not a pastor, but I feel it is my duty and obligation to warn pastors. The church is being co-opted. Eschatology buffs can debate about Roman Catholics from Western Europe and Muslims from the Middle East, but this *methodology*, in my opinion, points us to where the Bible says we are going. Where there is smoke there is fire.

The Emergent Church

The Emergent Church openly embraces the methodology of post-modernity (the Dialectic). More specifically, the Emergent movement embraces the philosophical assumptions underlying the Dialectical process. I had been researching this movement for less than an hour when I came to the following conclusion: *The Emergent Church is simply the syntheses of old liberal Christian theology and Eastern mysticism using Evangelical vocabulary.* The leadership in the Emergent Church (Brian McLaren, Richard Foster, Rob Bell, Tony Jones, etc.) openly challenges the virgin birth, hell, and the inerrancy of Scripture, among other things. Emergent theologians, conforming to the spirit of the age, teach that truth is not discovered (through a didactic reading of the Bible), but created through the communitarian process. In other words, murder isn't wrong because the Bible says it's wrong, murder is wrong because the social consensus of our day says it is wrong. But the social consensus of the day is subject to change, thus we see that the Emergent Church has given up on the idea of absolute truth. Belief doesn't correspond to reality, reality corresponds to belief.(2) The Emergent movement isn't seeking to transform the culture by being salt and light, it is being transformed by the culture through philosophical collectivism and the Dialectical methodology.

The Emergent Church espouses panentheism, that God is everywhere and in everything. This isn't outright pantheism because there is still some distinction between God and creation, but the line has been blurred.(3) (A transitional position perhaps?) Contemplative, mystical, experimental and experiential practices are encouraged. Brian McLaren celebrated Ramadan with Muslims in 2009, actually practicing the rituals of Islam.(4) To a Bible believing Christian, the Emergent Church is rationalized, systematic unbelief combined with flesh pleasing mysticism, plain and simple. It is accommodation to the spirit of the age (post-modernism) by Pastors and theologians who often seem to have an ax to grind when it comes to the fundamental doctrines of Evangelicalism.

At least with the Emergent Church, you know what you are getting. The movement is dangerous, of course, but at least it is transparent. Its philosophical position is well-defined and its intentions are clearly stated—to quote Rob Bell, "the rediscovery of Christianity as an Eastern Religion."(5) A new kind of Christian (who is no Christian at all).(6)

The Purpose Driven and Communitarian Church Growth Movements

The Purpose Driven and Communitarian Church Growth Movements are a little more tricky to deal with because you have to work a little harder to get to the bottom line. Clearly these two mega-movements use the dialectical methodology to market the church—to try to get people in the door. And that, of course, sounds like a good thing. (At least I can see how people can think it sounds like a good thing.) Pastors who use these techniques want to meet people where they are (to be seeker sensitive). Personally I would challenge the wisdom of this because, as I've already shown, the philosophical assumptions underlying this methodology are contrary to what we know from the Bible (Absolute Truth exists). In seeking to be relevant to the culture, slowly over time these churches absorb the culture while maintaining only a vague "christian" vocabulary. Sooner or later, these churches become irrelevant, the very thing they were trying to avoid all along. Why? Because they have nothing unique to offer. They are merely a reflection of the culture with a patina of spirituality. They have a form of godliness that denies the power of the Gospel. But let's do a little digging here.

Rick Warren was mentored by Peter Drucker, the father of modern management. Drucker taught that there are three sectors in society, the public sector (political), the private sector (economic), and the social sector (religious). Drucker is most widely known for his work in human management, in dealing with the public and private sectors. Using the Dialectical process (Total Quality Management), highly trained facilitators (leaders) learned to "guide" (manipulate) workers into going where leadership had already determined they needed to go, all the while making the process *feel* democratic. In the small group meeting, what you think and how you feel is encouraged. (It's kind of brilliant, really. Tyranny brought about via the democratic process.) But to the facilitator (change-agent), double-speak is a key tool. The uninitiated worker bees hear one thing, but leadership has another agenda in mind. To those who live in a black and white world this is called lying. With all of this in mind, the following quote from Aldous Huxley is pretty creepy:

"In the more efficient dictatorships of tomorrow there will probably be much less violence than under Hitler and Stalin. The future dictator's subjects will be painlessly regimented by a corps of highly trained social engineers."[7]

In the latter years of his life, Drucker recognized that the greatest potential for social transformation lies largely latent in the social sector (the religious sector). Drucker's three sectors became Warren's now famous three-legged stool. Warren discusses Drucker's writings with his staff and has visible reminders of his mentor's philosophy in his office at Saddleback. Warren views himself as a CEO-like Pastor and the people of his flock as customers and non-customers (believers and non-believers).[8] An article published by The Leadership Network, also heavily influenced by Drucker, records:

"Both Drucker and (Bob) Buford recognized the potential of these churches to re-energize Christianity in this country and to address societal issues that neither the public nor the private sector have been ableto resolve. The pastoral mega churches that have beengrowing so very fast in the US since the 1980s are surely the most important phenomenon in American society in the last 30 years."[9]

The question for me at this point is this: Are we dealing with foolish, although well-intended marketing of the church, or is something more insidious going on here? I think this quote from researcher/author Berit Kjos is sufficiently unambigous:

> "Today (the dialectical methodology is) the center-piece of all the world's management systems. Its purpose—which is *not* to nurture God's people—is to conform all minds to a global pattern for uniform 'human resource development' in schools, business, governments *and churches* around the world." (emphasis added) (10)

Drucker stated publicly many times that he was not a Christian. So it is safe to say that Drucker's agenda was not the Kingdom agenda. So question number one is this: If Drucker was no Christian, why would he be so interested in helping Warren's allegedly Evangelical agenda? Drucker was an intellectual of such a caliber that he would have easily recognized that the philosophical basis of his management methodology was antithetical to Biblical Christianity. (Salvation is collective, not individual; relative truth, not absolute truth; man-centered, not God-centered; etc.) In a philosophical paper written for *Forbes Magazine*, Drucker explicitly stated that there is no Natural Law (Absolute Truth) in the social (religious) universe. In light of what has already been said, the full quote is alarming:

> "The social universe has no 'natural laws' as the physical sciences do. It is thus subject to continuous change. This means that assumptions that were valid yesterday can become invalid and, indeed, totally misleading in no time at all."(11)

Warren is aware of these things as he has received literally thousands of warning letters. Many individuals report that they have received personal responses from Pastor Warren. Others even report that they were offered an expense paid visit to Saddleback Church (where I'm assuming they were to be "processed").

If it all stopped here, this would be, for me personally, plenty of reason for me to distance myself from the teachings of Saddleback, Purpose Driven, and Rick Warren. But it doesn't stop here.

Warren uses as many as 15 Bible versions in his books and sermons. If you take an hour to look at how he uses Scripture, which verses he uses, and when he uses them (I did this), a general trend soon emerges. He often uses softened, watered-down versions that make the verse more palatable. Rather than cite specific examples I encourage readers to research this themselves to see whether or not what I am saying is so. Warren's personal explanation is that he believes you communicate most effectively when you communicate most simply. But I go back to the double-speak that is used in Dr. Drucker's Total Quality Management. The potential for deception this creates is starting to seem like more than a coincidence. Maybe that's why Warren could get on Larry King Live and lie about his position and past statements concerning proposition 8, a 2008 ballot proposition dealing with the definition of marriage in California. (Watch this video that catches Warren red-handed. It's not a hit piece either, it's just Warren blatantly lying.)(12)

http://www.youtube.com/watch?v=xrEMRDOL-4g&feature=youtu.be

In public speeches to non-believing audiences, Warren repeatedly fails to give a clear gospel presentation. He says he wants people from all of the world's religions to work together to address pressing global issues like poverty, disease, illiteracy, corruption, and human trafficking. All important causes, to say the least, but they are all indicators that point to greater spiritual realities—the falleness of the world, the sinfulness of man, and mankind's need for a savior. If we give a hungry soul a loaf of bread but leave him without the gospel, his belly is full for an hour or two, yet his soul is still on its way to hell. Nobody in his right mind opposes social justice (the non-communitarian definition) and increasing the quality of life for people, but these causes have been co-opted to forward a collectivist, socialist agenda out of the United Nation's playbook; yet Christians think it is a play out of the Kingdom oriented, Biblical playbook. The fact that Warren and the people who speak at his events use globalist buzz words like sustainable development and the common good is a dead give away as to which side of the ledger America's Pastor is on. Warren does not make it a priority to discuss sin, repentance, hell, wrath, or even the resurrection. If someone can present me with evidence to the contrary, I would like to see it.

Rick Warren also brings known New Agers and Eastern mystics into his church. He has even endorsed writings that blatantly promote the occult. (Google the Daniel Plan, Dr. Oz, and Leonard Sweet if you want to see just three recent examples. Warren is promoting each of these.) In fact, in *Purpose-Driven Life*, Rick Warren begins day one by quoting Colossians 1:16, using The Message Bible, which replaces the phrase *in the Heavens and on earth* with *above and below*.(13) In light of what we already know, this seems a likely allusion to the well-known New Age/occult phrase "as above so below." Ronald S. Miller of *New Age Journal* explains the importance of this teaching:

"As above, so below; as below, so above.' This maxim implies that the transcendent God beyond the physical universe and the immanent God *within ourselves* are one."(emphasis added) (14)

Is it only a coincidence that Peter Drucker once wrote:

"(Mankind) needs the deep experience that the Thou and the I are one, which all higher religions share."(15)

At some point you have to stop giving a guy the benefit of the doubt. The evidence tells me that Rick Warren is a change agent who is preparing the church to accept a new global spirituality. Eddie Gibbs, senior professor of church growth in the School of Intercultural Studies at Fuller Theological Seminary spells it out in a crystal clear way:

"The church itself will need to go through a metamorphosis in order to find its new identity in the dialect of Gospel and Culture."(16)

That is a shockingly explicit statement. I respect the honesty. Use the Dialectical process to transition the church towards a transformational moment. Dr. Robert E. Klenck summarizes how this process works:

"In this movement, it is imperative that unbelievers be brought into the church; otherwise, the process of continual change cannot begin. There must be an antithesis (unbelievers) present to oppose the thesis (believers), in order to move towards consensus (compromise), and move the believers away from their moral absolutism (resistance to change). If all members of the church stand firm on the Word of God, and its final authority in all doctrine and tradition, then the church cannot and will not change. This is common faith. Soon we will see why these 'change agents' are pushing so hard for change to occur in the church."(17)

Why else would Rick Warren sit on the advisory board of the Tony Blair Faith Foundation, an organization with the stated purpose of bringing together all of the world's religion's under one umbrella? Consider the following quote from Rick Warren:

"The future of the world is not secularism, it's religious pluralism."(18)

While I agree that the statement is probably true, Warren said nothing to indicate that Christianity is not compatible with the coming pluralism.

Could this be why Warren is a member of the Council on Foreign Relations—an organization founded and funded using Rockefeller dollars with the stated goal of establishing a global communitarian system. Almost prophetically, John D Rockefeller, Jr. once said:

"I see the Church molding the thought of the world, as it has never done before, leading in all great movements as it should. I see it literally establishing the Kingdom of God on earth."(19)

Was Rockefeller a Christian concerned with the Kingdom of God? No, of course not. He simply identified the church as a vehicle he could co-opt and leverage with the family fortune. He was saying that the New World Order would ride in on the back of the apostate church. The woman riding the beast. Big government in bed with big business *under the umbrella of big religion*. While the religious right continues to beat the dead horses of liberals and the main stream media, it is being co-opted from within by the likes of Rick Warren, Rob Bell, and Brian McLaren.

I have to admit I am stunned by how far along this agenda is. Tony Blair stepped down as British Prime Minister, immediately converted to Roman Catholicism, and dedicated the rest of his life to bringing about a new world religion. Newt Gingrich, a 2012 GOP Presidential candidate and confirmed 33rd degree Freemason, also recently became a Roman Catholic. So much for the alleged enmity between the Vatican and Freemasons. That would help to explain how the World Council of Churches (funded by Rockefeller dollars and run by Freemasons), the Pontifical Council for Interreligious Dialogue, and the World Evangelical Alliance co-produced a document that includes a list of recommendations which basically say evangelization is a no-no in the brave new world.[20] It would help to explain why Rick Warren and Bill Hybels signed "the Yale document," as it has come to be known, which emphasizes the common ground between Islam and Christianity and talks as though the two faiths share the same God.[21]

But let's come back to the real world that most of us live in. Most Purpose Driven and Communitarian Church Growth fellowships strongly encourage participation in small groups.

I am not opposed to a small group in and of itself, of course, but I am highly interested in how the small groups are being used within the greater context of the church. Has the small group leader been trained (by Willow Creek) to be a leader (facilitator) to teach the Bible dialectically (as opposed to didactically)? In other words, is the group coming to the study to stand under the authority of the Bible and what it actually teaches, or is the group using dialogue (what everybody thinks and how everybody feels, felt needs) to arrive at a consensus. Is the consensus predetermined by the leader-facilitator? Remember that seeker sensitive marketing of the church introduces unbelievers into the church and these unbelievers are bringing their extra-Biblical worldviews into the small group. Once the process of change begins it continues without end, because the consensus of today (synthesis) is the thesis of tomorrow. Truth is a moving target on a pitching deck.

We live in an era where Biblical illiteracy prevails. Many pastors don't believe the Bible is God's authoritative Word anymore. When I was in seminary, I took a "leadership" course in which I was taught this dialectical methodology. They didn't call it that, of course, but that's what it was—even though I didn't recognize it at the time. During that class I was introduced to a man who was presented as a potential mentor figure. The first day I met him he told me that he didn't believe the entire Bible was inerrant in the original manuscripts. At that moment I decided having a mentor was not one of my high priorities. This is the watershed issue that Francis Schaeffer described—the inerrancy of the Word of God.[22] (John Loeffler's great flying wedge.) Some researchers in this area are admittedly over the top. They say your church is of the devil because you have greeters at the door, have a worship team, and allow women to wear pants. These are didactic bullies (pharisees) who lack common sense and undermine their own cause. On the other hand, I fear there are pastors who realize they have fallen for a deception, yet they are too invested and too prideful to publicly admit that they have been wrong. This is unacceptable for those who have been granted positions of authority within the Body of Christ.

Pastors, please renounce Rick Warren, Bill Hybels and their Purpose Driven church growth techniques. I will not fill out the connection cards or the spiritual gift assessments unless I can be assured that the data is not being used to provide a feedback loop that allows the church's spiritual progress to be evaluated, transitioned, and transformed. We can sensitively seek the lost, but we don't need to be seeker sensitive to the point that the unbelievers outnumber the believers two or three to one. The philosophies of the world can stay outside while we stand upon the inerrant, inspired, Spirit-breathed Word of God on the inside. Unity at all costs is compromise. Sometimes it is necessary to overturn the money tables in the temple complex. Right now is one of those times.

Persecution usually arrives suddenly. One day soon the apostate church will show us all which side we are really on. [End of essay]

In the final chapter, we'll look at the events that are likely to catalyze the great separation that I believe is coming very soon.

But first, let's add a few more lines to *The Omega Manifesto*:

33) The Emergent Church / Purpose Driven / Church Growth movements have brought the Dialectical process into the church and are to be renounced.

34) The Word of God, illuminated by the Holy Spirit, is our source of Absolute Truth. This is a non-negotiable.

35) Persecution is coming to the church in America and the West.

Chapter 9 Endnotes

(1) John Loeffler, Rethinking Good Church vs. Bad Church. http:// www.steelonsteel.com/2008/01/19/rethinking-good-church-vs-bad-church/—accessed July 18, 2011.

(2) Jason Carlson, "On His Journey In and Out of the Emergent Church," video on Worldview Tube. http://worldviewweekend.com/worldview-tube/video.php?videoid=1810 accessed July 18, 2011.

(3) Understanding the Times with Jan Markell radio broadcast, 03/12/2011, hour two, guest host Brannon Howse. OTM2011_03_12B.mp3, radio archives—accessed July 18, 2011.

(4) Joel Richardson, " 'Christians' Celebrating Ramadan?", Worldnetdaily, August 25, 2009. http://www.wnd.com/index.php?fa= PAGE.view&pageId=107812—accessed July 18, 2011.

(5) Andy Crouch, *The Emergent Mystique*. Christianity Today, 11/01/2004. http://www.christianitytoday.com/ct/2004/november/12.36.html —accessed July 18, 2011.

(6) To borrow from the title of Brian McLaren's book, *A New Kind of Christianity*.

(7) Aldous Huxley, *Brave New World Revisited*, (New York: Harper & Row, 1958), 26.

(8) Understanding the Times with Jan Markell radio broadcast, 11/20/2011, hour two, guest host Brannon Howse. OTM2010_11_20B.mp3, radio archives accessed—July 18, 2011.

(9) Leadership Network Feature, November 14, 2005. http://www.pursuantgroup.com/leadnet/advance/nov05o.htm—accessed July 18, 2011.

(10) Barit Kjos, *Spirit-Led or Purpose-Driven? Part 3—Small Groups and the Dialectic Process*.

http://www.crossroad.to/articles2/04/3-purpose.htm—accessed July 18, 2011.

(11) Peter Drucker, *Management's New Paradigms*. Forbes Magazine, October 5, 1998.
http://www.forbes.com/forbes/1998/1005/6207152a_print.html—accessed July 18, 2011.

(12) Good Fight Ministries YouTube Channel, *Rick Warren's Forked Tongue*.
http://www.youtube.com/watch?v=xrEMRDOL-4g&feature=youtu.be—accessed July 18, 2011.

(13) Rick Warren, *The Purpose-Driven Life*, (Grand Rapids: Zondervan, 2002), 17.

(14) Warren Smith, *Excerpts from Deceived on Purpose*
http://www.crossroad.to/articles2/04/smith-deceived_on_purpose.htm—accessed July 19, 2011.

(15) Peter Drucker, *Landmarks of Tomorrow*, (New York: Harper & Brothers,1959), 264-265.

(16) Cameron Crabtree, *Church growth scholar advocates radical change in new millennium.*(BaptistPress.org, November 23, 1998).
http://www.baptistpress.org/bpnews.asp?ID=4888—accessed July 19, 2011.

(17) Dr. Robert E. Klenck, M.D., *How Diaprax Manifests Itself in the Church.*
http://www.crossroad.to/News/Church/Klenck3.html—accessed July 19, 2011.

(18) *A New Century, A New Reformation.* Washington National Cathedral Website, January 27, 2008.
http://www.nationalcathedral.org/events/SF080127.shtml—accessed July 19, 2011.

(19) The American Review of Reviews, Edited by Albert Shaw, (New York: The Review of Reviews Company, 1919), 202.

(20) *Christian Witness in a Multi-Religious World, Recommendations for Conduct.*
http://www.cbcisite.com/Recommendations%20for%20Conduct.pdf —accessed July 19, 2011.

(21) *Loving God and Neighbor Together, A Christian Response to "A Common Word Between Us and You."*
http://www.yale.edu/faith/acw/acw.htm—accessed July 19, 2011.

(22) Francis A. Shaeffer, *The Great Evangelical Disaster*, (Wheaton, IL: Crossway Books, 1984), 44.

Chapter 10—Days of Noah

Between 2005 and 2007 I had a website called DaysofNoah.org. When I named the site and registered my domain name, I frankly had no idea what I was doing. I took the name from the well-known passage Luke 17:26:

> *And just as it happened in the days of Noah, so it will be also in the days of the Son of Man.*

In the West, we don't necessarily understand or appreciate the value and the power that is in a name. In the East, and in the Hebraic culture from which the Bible originated, the importance and the power of a name was and is more readily understood.[1] I believe the name I picked for my website played a role in my discovering what I am about to share. It may seem that in this chapter I am indulging in a flight of fancy, but for reasons that will become evident by the end of the chapter, I feel the inclusion of this material in *The Omega Manifesto* is absolutely essential.

Luke 17:27 describes what happened in the days of Noah (Luke 17:26):

> *. . . They were eating, they were drinking, they were marrying, they were being given in marriage, until*

---

[6]The Bible is best understood within the context of the Hebrew culture from which it derives. In this way many aspects of Eastern culture, foreign to the West, actually prove quite helpful.

the day that Noah entered the ark, and the flood came and destroyed them all.

The most obvious meaning here is that for Noah's generation it was business as usual right up until the moment the deluge began. Noah had warned the people the flood was coming, but the stubborn world refused to pay attention to the prophetic forecast and they were consequently destroyed in the flood. In this historical account we see that God is gracious and long-suffering, not wanting any to perish, but at some point His patience runs out. In a similar way, Luke is telling us that in the days just prior to the return of Jesus Christ it will be business as usual for the earth-dwellers. They will have been warned by those pointing to the Biblical fulfillment of eschatological prophecies, but many will refuse to heed these warnings and will reject the Gospel of Christ. Only this time the unbelieving world will not be destroyed by water, as in the Days of Noah, it will be destroyed by fire, as described in 2 Peter 3:3-7:

> *Know this first of all, that in the last days mockers will come with their mocking, following after their own lusts, and saying, "Where is the promise of His coming? For ever since the fathers fell asleep, all continues just as it was from the beginning of creation." For when they maintain this, it escapes their notice that by the word of God the heavens existed long ago and the earth was formed out of water and by water, through which the world at that time was destroyed, being flooded with water. But by His word the present heavens and earth are being reserved for fire, kept for the day of judgment and destruction of ungodly men.*

But notice that in Luke 17:27 Jesus says *they were marrying* and *they were being given in marriage*. Let's look at the account of Noah, starting in Genesis 6:1:

> *Now it came about, when men began to multiply on the face of the land, and daughters were born to them, that **the sons of God** saw that the daughters of men were beautiful; and **they took wives for themselves**, whomever they chose.*

Elsewhere in the Old Testament the phrase the sons of God refers to angels (see Job 1:6; 2:1; 38:7). So what this text is saying, strange as it may seem, is that some of the angels of Heaven took human women as their wives.

With this in mind, the text of Genesis 6 continues:

> *The Nephilim were on the earth in those days, and also afterward, when the sons of God came in to the daughters of men, and they bore children to them. Those were the mighty men who were of old, men of renown.*

The plain meaning of the text is that the angels and the women had intercourse and gave birth to hybrid offspring which were half human and half angel. That's who the Nephilim were. All of the sudden Jesus' words in Luke take an intriguing prophetic turn:

> *And just as it happened in the days of Noah, so it will be also in the days of the Son of Man; they were eating, they were drinking, they were marrying, they were being given in marriage, until the day that*

Noah entered the ark, and the flood came and destroyed them all.

The account of Noah in Genesis specifically tells us that not only were people getting married, but that some of the women were marrying angels and having hybrid offspring. If we take the texts of Genesis and Luke at face value, the implication is that that this business with the Nephilim will be happening *again* in the last days just prior to the second coming of Jesus Christ. Many who oppose this view point to the fact that Jesus said that angels in *heaven* neither marry nor are given in marriage. Of course, but some of the angels sinned and came *to earth*. Jude, a book that often gets overlooked as people rush to get to Revelation, provides additional and important insights in this regard:

> *And angels who did not keep their own domain, but abandoned their proper abode, He has kept in eternal bonds under darkness for the judgment of the great day, just as Sodom and Gomorrah and the cities around them, since they **in the same way** as these indulged in gross immorality and **went after strange flesh**, are exhibited as an example in undergoing the punishment of eternal fire.* (Jude 6-7)

The meaning of this is clear. The angels found a way to "disrobe" from their unfallen, perfect heavenly bodies in order to be able to copulate with the human women. One has to play games and do theological gymnastics with the clear meaning of the text to get around this. Just as Sodom and Gomorrah was judged for sexual perversion (among other things), so too were these angels that sinned, who *indulged in gross immorality and went after strange flesh*. For this reason, Jude tells us, the angels are being held in temporary hell until judgment day. In fact, let's take a moment to go down that rabbit hole, as it will help to crystallize where we are heading.

Hell

Many Christians may be surprised to learn that the Bible contains at least six different words that are, loosely speaking, translated into English as "Hell." (Recall that the Bible was written in Hebrew, Aramaic, and Koine Greek.) The Old Testament term for Hell is Sheol (Hebrew), which is often incorrectly interpreted as "the grave." New Testament words used for Hell are more diverse, including Hades, the Abyss, the Pit/Bottomless Pit, Tartarus, and Gehenna. All of these words have been translated as Hell by competent translators and commentators. So what gives? Are all six Biblical words referring to the same place? Are there six different Hells? Are we missing something here? Well, there are not six different Hells, yet all six words are not referring to the same place.

First of all, the Old Testament word Sheol (Hebrew— שְׁאוֹל) and the New Testament Hades (Greek—αδηχ) are essentially equivalent. The Hebrew Lexicon of the Blue Letter Bible defines Sheol thus:

> Hades, a subterranean place full of thick darkness (Job 10:21, 22) in which the shades [spirits] of the dead are gathered together.(1)

The word Hades appears 11 times in the New Testament. Ten times it is translated Hell. Only in 1 Corinthians 15:55 is Hades translated death.

The word Gehenna appears 12 times in the New Testament and is always translated as Hell. However, I do not believe that Hades and Gehenna are synonymous. First of all, here is a bit of background on Gehenna: Originally a location southwest of Jerusalem where children were burned as sacrifices to the god Molech, Gehenna later became a garbage dump with a continuous burning of trash.(2) In Bible times therefore, Gehenna was used to illustrate the abode of the damned in Jewish theology. Gehenna is mentioned in Mark 9:43 and following and also in Matthew 10:28 as the place of punishment and unquenchable fire where both the body and soul of the wicked go after death. It is also apparently the future abode of Satan and his angels (Matt. 25:41).

As I already stated, I believe Hades and Gehenna are technically different localities. Revelation 20:13-14 provides a major clue:

The sea gave up the dead that were in it, and death and Hades gave up the dead that were in them, and each person was judged according to what he had done. Then death and Hades were thrown into the lake of fire. The lake of fire is the second death.

It seems as though Hades/Sheol is a temporary holding place for the damned pending the Great White Throne Judgment (Revelation 20:11-15). This is further supported by 1 Peter 3:19; 2 Peter 2:4 and Jude 6, which together describe a temporary holding place for the angels that sinned (cf. Genesis 6). Hades/Sheol then is the location of "temporary" Hell (1 Peter 3:19) while Gehenna is the location of eternal Hell.

But I believe we can be even more specific. Three times Jesus describes outer darkness (Gehenna) as the future fate of unbelievers—Matthew 8:12; Matthew 22:13; and Matthew 25:30. During the period between His death and resurrection, Jesus descended into the heart of the earth—Matthew 12:40; Psalm 88; 1 Peter 3:19, 4:6. It seems rather as if Hades (temporary Hell), in the heart of the earth, will be emptied into Gehenna (permanent Hell), in outer darkness (Revelation 20:13-14).

So we've talked about Sheol, Hades, and Gehenna. But what of the Bottomless Pit, the Abyss, and Tartarus? It appears as though these three locations are sub-regions of Hades (or Sheol, temporary Hell). The Bottomless Pit / Abyss is mentioned seven times in the book of Revelation. This may sound strange, but if one is residing in the center of a sphere (i.e. the heart of the earth where Hades is), theoretically the only direction to go is up—hence Bottomless Pit (although there could be some dimensionality factors in play here too). Simply put, the Bottomless Pit / Abyss is the lower region of Hades, the lowest hell of Deuteronomy 32:22:

> *For a fire is kindled in mine anger, and shall burn unto **the lowest hell**, and shall consume the earth with her increase, and set on fire the foundations of the mountains.*

This brings us to 2 Peter 2:4 (this chapter parallels the aforementioned Book of Jude), where Peter writes:

> *For if God spared not the angels that sinned, but cast them down to hell, and delivered them into chains of darkness, to be reserved unto judgment. . . .*

These angels that sinned are the same that Jude references (those who fooled around with human women resulting in hybrid offspring). But the word Peter uses here for hell is the Greek word Tartaroo, which comes from the root word Tartarus (Greek ταρταροσ)—defined by Strong's Concordance as "the deepest abyss of Hades."[3]

What we have learned then, is that Sheol/Hades is the temporary place of incarceration for wicked souls—pending the Great White Throne Judgment (Revelation 20:11-15). After that great prophetic event, the damned will be moved from Hades in the heart of the earth and placed eternally in the outer darkness of Gehenna (the lake of fire). Furthermore, Biblically we can say with some confidence that there are degrees of judgment for the wicked just like there are different levels of reward for the righteous (Luke 20:47; 1 Corinthians 3:11-15). Thus it seems as though the Bottomless Pit, Abyss and Tartarus correspond to the lower regions of Hades/Sheol.

Some scholars believe that after Jesus' resurrection Abraham's Bosom (Paradise) was moved from the heart of the earth to the highest Heaven where our Lord has His throne. (A temporary Paradise verses a permanent Heaven.) Whether this is accurate or not, Biblical Hell—at least in the way we classically think of it—is Gehenna whereas Hades is the underworld in the heart of the earth (as described—with varying degrees of accuracy—in all of the ancient mythologies, Dante's Inferno, etc.).

The most important fact to remember, however, is that anyone who seeks to enter Heaven by any other way other than through repentance and a personal relationship with the Lord Jesus Christ will spend eternity in the torment of Hell (outer darkness), which is a very real place.

Let us return now to the Nephilim and the Days of Noah. The Bible isn't the only source that talks about these ancient hybrid creatures. The pseudoepigraphal Book of Enoch (this just means that it was written under a pseudonym, or a false name) says of these strange entities:

> "Enoch, thou scribe of righteousness, go, declare to the Watchers of the heavens who have left the high heaven, the holy eternal place, and have defiled themselves with women, and have done as the children of earth do, and have taken unto themselves wives: 'Ye have wrought great destruction on the earth: And ye shall have no peace nor forgiveness of sin: and inasmuch as they delight themselves in their children [the hybrid offspring, the Nephilim], The murder of their beloved ones shall they see, and over thedestruction of their children shall they lament, and shall make supplication unto eternity, but mercy and peace shall ye not attain."(1 Enoch 12:3-6)

Interestingly, the Bible mentions a city named Shinar (located in modern day Iraq). Shinar literally means land of the Watchers, and this is the place from which the ancient Egyptians originally migrated. (The Watchers were those who fathered these Nephilim.) The destruction of the Nephilim spoken of in the Book of Enoch occurred in the Great Flood. It is worth mentioning that many bright Bible scholars and teachers talk about fallen angels and demons interchangeably, as if they are the same thing. I do not believe this view to be correct. In the Scriptures angels, fallen or not, have a body and can even be indistinguishable from humans. Demons, on the other hand, are always seeking a body to inhabit and cannot (usually) be seen with the naked human eye. I believe that demons are the disembodied spirits of these Nephilim hybrids (some of whom seem to have been giants) that were physically killed in the flood (and also after). The Apocryphal Book of Jubilees (aka the Apocalypse of Moses) confirms this:

> "And in the third week of this jubilee the vile demons began to lead astray the sons of Noah and deceived them and destroyed them. And the sons came to Noah their father and told him concerning the demons which were leading astray, darkening, and slaying the sons of their sons. And he prayed before the Lord his God and he said, 'Lord of the spirits of all flesh thou hast shown mercy to me and hast delivered me and my children from the waters of the deluge, and hast not suffered me to be destroyed as thou didst the children of destruction, for thy grace was great over men, and great was thy mercy over my soul; may thy grace be exalted over the sons of their sons, and may the evil spirits not rule over them to destroy the earth. And thou hast verily blessed me and my sons that we increase and multiply and fill the earth. And thou knowest how the **Watchmen**, the father of these spirits, acted in my day; and these spirits also which are alive, cast them into prison and hold them in the places of judgment." (Jubilees 10:1-5)

This says that the Watchmen (another way of saying Watchers) were the fathers of these evil spirits or demons. Notice also the possible allusion to the places of judgment mentioned in Jude 6-7, 2 Peter 2:4, and Deuteronomy 32:22.

Even the Dead Sea Scrolls testify to the veracity of the accounts recording ancient Nephilim on earth. Tom Horn writes in *Nephilim Stargates*:

"According to the Dead Sea Scrolls, only two hundred of this larger group of powerful beings called 'Watchers' departed from the higher Heavens and sinned. Thus, Enoch refers to the Watchers in the High Heavens as separate from the ones on earth. The fallen class of Watchers are considered by some to be the 'angels which kept not their first estate, but left their own habitation . . . [and are] reserved in everlasting chains under darkness unto judgment of the great day.' "(4)

Not only do Biblical and extra-Biblical texts confirm the reality of these hybrid offspring, so too do many of the mythologies of the ancient world. Chuck Missler and Mark Eastman write in their book *Alien Encounters*:

"In fact, the existence of flying humanoid 'gods' who came to Earth, interacted with and even interbred with mankind, are found extensively in the literature of ancient Egypt, Greece, the Incas, Mayas, Hindus, Native Americans, and others."(5)

Many of the ancient Church Fathers corroborated this view, including Justin Martyr, Irenaeus, Clement of Alexandria, and Tertullian just to name a few.(6) Historians Josephus Flavius and Philo also throw the weight of their support behind this interpretation.(7)

It is important to add that one cannot truly understand the Great Flood apart from the gene-pool problem that was created by the hybrid program and the genetic tampering that went on just prior to the flood (and after). We'll return to this in a moment, but for now consider Jesus' words in Luke again:

> *And just as it happened in the days of Noah, so it will be also in the days of the Son of Man.*

The clear implication is that the foolishness of Genesis 6 will be going on *again* in the days just prior to Jesus' return.

Much more could be written about the existence of the Nephilim in the ancient world and how they manifested as giants even after the flood. I could get into a massive archaeological cover-up that has concealed important findings in this regard. I could talk about how the genetic tampering that occurred in the Days of Noah was not merely limited to the angel and human realms, but it spilled over into the animal and plant kingdoms as well (Jasher 4:18). But the people who aren't going to believe it aren't going to believe it no matter what I write. This is not meant to be an exhaustive treatment as many competent writers have already covered this ground.

Days of Noah II

In 1918, Aleister Crowley (the Father of the New Age movement and modern culture), conducted a metaphysical experiment which came to be known as the Amalantrah Working. Through this occult ritual, Crowley created a dimensional portal through which an entity very much resembling an alien grey was said to have come through. Then in 1947 L. Ron Hubbard (who founded the Church of Scientology) and Jack Parsons (of the Jet Propulsion Laboratory) imitated Crowley's ritual in an attempt to create a "moon child" that would "incarnate the whore of Babylon."(8) The pair called their ritual the Babalon Working. Intriguingly, 1947 was the year that Aleister Crowley died and is also widely held to be the year ufologists say worldwide UFO sightings began to dramatically increase. As a matter of fact, the controversial Roswell incident occurred in 1947. Is it merely a coincidence that the opening of the Babylon Working dimensional portal coincided with the sudden manifestation of UFO and "alien" phenomena?

To those in the know, the interdimensional character of UFOs and their mysterious inhabitants is well documented. The unknown craft have been observed to materialize and dematerialize—often very quickly. What's more, the shape of the aircraft will often morph or even break up into several pieces. In this regard, I find the following illustration, which I first heard from Chuck Missler, to be very helpful.

Think of a two-dimensional being living in a two-dimensional world—say, a piece of paper. The 2D being can hardly conceive of the 3D world that we know so well because he is locked up in two dimensions. Now say that you, as a 3D being, want to mess with the poor chap in the 2D world. Holding your four fingers together (excluding your thumb), you dip your hand through the 2D plane (represented by the piece of paper) down to about your knuckles (via a hypothetical portal). To the 2D being, your 3D fingers will look roughly like four 2D circles all pressed in together forming a row. As you move your fingers up and down through the plane, the circles will vary in size (morph) according to the thickness of your fingers as they move through the 2D "window" in the 2D world. But if you suddenly decided to rapidly spread your fingers wide apart, the singular object, to the 2D being, would appear to break into four separate objects. Your fingers would still be connected to your hand of course, but to the 2D being it would look as if four separate objects had "magically" formed.

In a similar way, could beings from a dimensionality beyond space-time be messing with us through three-dimensional "windows" in our universe? Although they must be inferred indirectly, modern mathematics has enabled us to prove the existence of at least 10 dimensions. Time itself has physical properties and physicists consider time to be the fourth dimension. You will notice scientists using the term space-time (not space *and* time) precisely because of this reality. To quote Chuck Missler,

> "Time is now known to be a physical property that varies with mass, acceleration, and gravity."[9]

So we have the four dimensions of space-time (Ephesians 3:18?) and the six hyperspaces that can be mathematically inferred. (Light may be a vibration in the fifth dimension.) Then we have the spiritual realms which somehow interface with these dimensions in ways just beyond normal human perception. God has put a dimensional veil in place, as it were, but since 1947 beings and their aircraft have found ways to breech this veil and to manifest in space-time.

This is not to say that the beings and their aircraft exhibit *no* physical properties. They are often picked up by radar, leave behind physical evidence like craters, scorched earth, or even radiation.[10] In this way we can rightly say that "UFOs behave as both natural and supernatural phenomenon."[11] These craft seem to defy the known laws of physics. For example, they have been observed to travel at 25,000 miles per hour without burning up in the atmosphere, have made right angle turns at 15,000 mph, and, despite these amazing velocities, they do not create a sonic boom.(12)

With the appearance of these UFOs and the paradoxes they confront us with, are we also witnessing "the appearance of a new paradigm of thought—one in which the lines separating faith and science, religion, philosophy, the material world, and the spirit world are [being] blurred"?(13) Are the UFO/extraterrestrial narratives deliberate misdirection intended to prepare the way for the coming new (false) paradigm of the New World Order?

While these Satanic beings may pose as our extraterrestrial progenitors from the Pleiades, having returned to guide us through a coming quantum leap in our own evolution, even secular ufologists are skeptical as to their actual agenda. Many have rightly connected these alleged "aliens" to the Biblical phenomena of angels and demons. While there are of course ridiculous and easily debunked tales of alien encounters on the internet, there are far too many intelligent, otherwise normal people reporting astonishingly consistent accounts of being abducted by non-human beings. In short, I believe these beings and their craft are more interdimensional than intergalactic. This is the reason I mentioned Gap Theory in chapter three. Steve Quayle, among others, believes that there was a pre-Adamic society on earth that was judged, which would explain the destruction described in Genesis 1:2. Could it be that this civilization extended out into the solar system and even beyond into other parts of the galaxy? Could it be that during this epoch in the history of the universe, the dimensional veil did not exist? In this sense then, could it be accurate that these beings really *are* intergalactic/extraterrestrial, though they have now been relegated to the spiritual realm? This is one of the reasons I am open to Gap Theory as what I am describing *may* be a part of the end time delusion that will deceive even the elect if it were possible. (I am not asserting it dogmatically, I am merely saying that I am open to the possibility.) It could be that one of the objectives behind the modern day Genesis-six-like hybrid program (which according to my sources began in earnest in 1949) is to produce fake ETs who will deceive the world. (More on this in a moment.) One can certainly see the scripting, the PR roll-outs, and the trial balloons as humanity is slowly being conditioned to accept the soon-coming disclosure of life beyond ourselves in the cosmos.

I believe the rainbow that represents the covenant given to Noah after the flood may represent something more than the fact that God would not destroy the world again with a global flood (see Genesis 9). The rainbow represents the spectrum of light which is visible to the naked eye. And yet we know that visible light comprises only a sliver of the electromagnetic spectrum. To the extreme left of the spectrum one can find long-waves, which have electromagnetic radiation with a measurable wavelength of literally thousands of kilometers. To the extreme right of the spectrum are gamma rays, which have a wavelength that can be measured at sizes a fraction of the diameter of a single atom. When God said let there be light on the first day of creation, He was creating much more than merely the visible electromagnetic spectrum. Could the rainbow be, therefore, a visible representation of a dimensional veil being put in place? Was God closing portals that had been breached in the creation of these hybrids of Genesis 6—portals like Mount Hermon and the Tower of

Babel? Isn't it interesting that in Revelation 6:2, the antichrist appears on a white horse holding a bow? Is this bow an allusion, as the Greek may indicate, to Noah's rainbow? If so, does this passage hint at the possibility that the dimensional veil has once again been fully breached by the time the antichrist comes on the scene? Whether this interpretation of Revelation 6:2 is accurate or not, I fully believe that the spiritual realm and the "natural" realm are on a collision course and that full disclosure is imminent. Go ahead and laugh at me now, but what are you going to do when you are standing face to face with a powerful fallen angel, demon, or hybrid entity (perhaps posing as a grey, a reptilian, a Nordic, or of course as an angel of Light)? How is the average human going to react when these supposedly illuminated beings start teaching us their demonic doctrines and foisting their highly deceptive Satanic agenda upon us?

If you study the messages that these "ETs" give to humanity, why do they seem so preoccupied with a one world government and a one world religion? Why do they seem to be towing the Green line while warning of World War III? Or, to put it succinctly as John Ankerberg and John Weldon do in *The Facts on UFOs and Other Supernatural Phenomena*:

> ". . . How credible is it to think that literally thousands of genuine extraterrestrials would fly millions or billions of light years simply to teach New Age philosophy, deny Christianity, and support the occult?"(14)

Could it be that these off-world entities are representatives of the evil spiritual realm that have been the impetus behind the New World Order all along? Or as Tom Horn brilliantly puts it in his ground-breaking book, *Apollyon Rising 2012*:

". . . Beyond the machinations of financiers and occult ideologues who direct global institutions—. . . behind their matrix of illusion—which most citizens perceive as reality—is an arena of evil supernatural-ism under which these human 'conduits' are will-ingly organized."(15)

Readers may be startled to realize that the New World Order—global government and a one world religion—is only a means to an end and not the actual end in and of itself. But if the NWO isn't the endgame, what is?

Endgame

Author and researcher Budd Hopkins has concluded that the beings are here "to carry out a complex breeding experi-ment in which they seem to be working to create a hybrid species, a mix of human and alien characteristics."(16)

Working on behalf of the Luciferian hierarchy, the elites in government, intelligence, the military, and the media have carefully concealed and covered up the truth about UFOs and so-called aliens. As Dr. Brian O'Leary (a former astronaut who has been a faculty member at UC Berkeley, Cornell, the California Institute of Technology, and Princeton) put it:

"Those who have investigated this hydra-headed beast of UFO, alien, *mind-control*, *genetic engineer-ing*, free energy, anti-gravity propulsion, and other secrets will make Watergate or Irangate appear to be kindergarten exercises." (emphasis added)(17)

It is common knowledge among those who research this kind of thing that victims of "alien"abductions often report having to endure humiliating examinations that revolve around sexual reproduction. In fact, many report having had sexual encounters with the entities! This is the same non-sense that went on back in Genesis 6!

> *Now it came about, when men began to multiply on the face of the land, and daughters were born to them, that the sons of God saw that the daughters of men were beautiful; and they took wives for them-selves, whomever they chose.*

For so long I just assumed that this type of activity was some bizarre form of perversion and rebellion against the natural created order. This is true, of course, but slowly over the last couple of years it has dawned on me that there is an agenda *behind* this bizarre hybrid/genetic engineering program.

Agenda #1—The "Creation" of Antichrist

As discussed in chapter 4, I believe the world may soon see the emergence of a scintillating world leader. This leader will meet the messianic expectations of Jews, Muslims, New Agers, and occultists alike. He will be a master geo-politician, a military genius, a hypnotic orator, and a supernatural miracle worker the likes of which the world has never seen. I believe he will be a human-angel hybrid and literally the "seed of Satan" (see Genesis 3:15).

There has recently emerged a school of thought that believes the antichrist will be a super-engineered and genetically enhanced being. In fact, many believe that the antichrist could be born human before "becoming" something quite different. Tom Horn is among those who have put forward this view, which he bases in large part on an interesting reading of Genesis 10:8. If correct, this passage would indeed establish a Biblical precedent for the science-fiction-like subject we have now broached.

> *Now Cush became the father of Nimrod; he became a mighty hunter before the Lord.*

Now the King James Version of the Bible translates the latter portion of this verse as *he began to be a mighty one in the earth.* According to the Blue Letter Bible, the Hebrew verb that is rendered *he began* (transliterated *chalal*) carries with it the connotation of something being profaned, defiled, or polluted. Of course, if Nimrod *[profanely] began to be a mighty one*, this implies that he wasn't always a mighty hunter. What's more, the word which is rendered in English as *mighty one* or *mighty hunter* is in the Hebrew *gibborim*, which is a word used synonymously with Nephilim in the aforementioned Genesis 6:

> *The Nephilim were on the earth in those days, **and also afterward**, when the sons of God came in to the daughters of men, and they bore children to them. Those were the **mighty men** who were of old, men of renown* (Genesis 6:4).

First, the phrase *mighty men* (*gibborim* in the Hebrew) grammatically refers back to the Nephilim mentioned earlier in the verse. Note also that we are told that the Nephilim were on the earth *in those days* [contemporaneously with the Great Flood], *and also afterward.* This means therefore that the Nephilim were on the earth *after* the flood. Joshua encountered giants in the land while David encountered Goliath and his five giant brothers. Importantly, the brutal nature of much of what we read in the Book of Joshua begins to make more sense when it is approached from the standpoint of this paradigm (cf. Numbers 13:33).

Let us now return to what was previously stated about the gene-pool problem that occurred in the days of Noah. This was, I would assert, *the* primary driver behind God's judgment that came in the form of the Great Flood. Simply put, Satan's transgenic strategy was to corrupt the human gene-pool to the point that it would not be possible for humanity to produced the "seed of the woman" (Genesis 3:15), that is, the promised Messiah. By preserving Noah and his family, God was preserving the line of that crucial seed. If this seems contrived, consider Genesis 6:9, which grammatically implies that Noah and his family had not been corrupted by the ongoing assault on human DNA.

> *Noah was a righteous man,* **blameless** *in his time.*

The Hebrew word translated as blameless implies completeness or wholeness. Translation: Noah's line had not been infected by the hybrid DNA. In fact, the King James renders the phrase *blameless in his time* as *perfect in his generations.* This is just another way of saying that his genealogy was unblemished. (Generations in this context means genealogy.) The completeness or wholeness of Noah's DNA stands in stark contrast to the other earth-dwellers:

Now the earth was corrupt in the sight of God, and the earth was filled with violence. God looked on the earth, and behold, it was corrupt; **for all flesh had corrupted their way upon the earth**. (Genesis 6:11-12)

Surely the corruption of the flesh here is an allusion to the genetic Pandora's box which had been opened through the human-angel hybrid program. So, does Genensis 10:8 reveal that Nimrod began to engange in this same pre-flood foolishness? Tom Horn summarizes an intriguing view:

"Therefore, in modern language, this text could accurately be translated to say: 'And Nimrod began to change genetically, becoming a gibborim, the offspring of watchers on earth.' "(18)

There may even be, according to Horn, a clue in the Book of Jubilees as to how Nimrod may have come across this knowledge and scientific know-how. Jubilees 8 records that one of Noah's grandsons stumbled onto some secret writings:

"And [Noah's grandson] grew, and his father taught him writing, and he went to seek for himself a place where he might seize for himself a city. And he found a writing which former (generations) had carved on the rock, and he read what was thereon, and he transcribed it and sinned owing to it; for it contained the teaching of **the Watchers** in accordance with which they used to observe the omens of the sun and moon and stars in all the signs of heaven. And he wrote it down and said nothing regarding it; for he was afraid to speak to Noah about it lest he should be angry with him on account of it." (Jubilees 8:2-5)

Remember that some of the Watchers were among those who abandoned their proper abode and came to earth to mingle with human women. Is it possible that the grandson of Noah who discovered this information concerning the Watchers, though he hid it from Noah, shared it with Nimrod (who would have been either a nephew or a son)? Is it possible that the antichrist will be born a human, but, through genetic engineering, biotechnology, nanotechnology, and occult ritual he will *begin to be* a *gibborim*—an entity that is no longer fully human? This is certainly a fantastic scenario.

Doug Riggs has critiqued this view of Genesis 10:8 and argues convincingly that it is based on an overly-broad reading of the verse. He states that the conclusions drawn from the word *gibborim* take unwarranted grammatical liberties with the text. (It is certainly true that we have to be careful about using a concordance as a lexicon.) Besides knowing Hebrew and Greek, Doug has worked with actual women who have given birth to these hybrid offspring. Based on their authoritative testimonies and consistent eye witness accounts, Doug assured me over the phone that no such genetic engineering or manipulation is necessary in real-life first generation hybrid offspring. In other words, according to Doug they are born with everything they need already in their DNA. In fact, there is a blonde-haired blue-eyed entity by the name of Nimrod Apollyon Alexander who is highly esteemed and considered a strong candidate to fill the roll of antichrist when the time comes.

Will the coming messiah of the New World Order be born a hybrid? Will he be born a human and subsequently undergo genetic transformation through nanotechnology, biotechnology, genetic engineering, and even occult ritual? Or will he perhaps be born a hybrid and under go further genetic modification? The shocking revelation is that all of these eventualities are both scientifically and technologically plausible. Based on my study of this strange subject, I lean towards Mr. Riggs' view that the antichrist will be *born* a hybrid as I strongly believe this is a key objective behind the hybrid program that is underway in our own time, just as it was in the days of Noah.

Only time will tell, but there is an overlooked verse at the end of Daniel 2 which provides yet another important clue. Prophetically, this passage unquestionably refers to the coming kingdom of antichrist (which will in some way be an extension of the ancient Roman Empire):

> "*And in that you saw the iron mixed with common clay, **they will combine with one another in the seed of men**; but they will not adhere to one another, even as iron does not combine with pottery.*"(Daniel 2:43)

The "they" in this passage seems to hint that the gibborim/Nephilim will in some way take part in the administration of the Kingdom of Antichrist. As Chuck Missler points out, to mingle with the seed of men they have to be something other than the seed of men.

Finally, in support of the hybrid view of the antichrist, at the end of the Book of Revelation we see that the Antichrist and the False Prophet are thrown alive into the Lake of Fire before the inauguration of the Millennial Kingdom and before the Great White Throne Judgment.

> *"And the beast was seized, and with him the false prophet who performed the signs in his presence, by which he deceived those who had received the mark of the beast and those who worshiped his image; these two were thrown alive into the lake of fire which burns with brimstone."* (Revelation 19:20)

This is curious because the souls of wicked humanity are judged at the Great White Throne *after* the Millennial Kingdom.

> *"And the sea gave up the dead which were in it, and death and Hades* [temporary hell] *gave up the dead which were in them; and they were judged, every one of them according to their deeds. Then death and Hades were thrown into the lake of fire. This is the second death, the lake of fire. And if anyone's name was not found written in the book of life, he was thrown into the lake of fire."* (Revelation 20:13-14)

Question: Why are the beast and false prophet thrown into the lake of fire a thousand years before the rest of humanity? I believe the answer is that the beast and false prophet are hybrid beings that are not fully human and therefore are not eligible to receive salvation through the efficacious blood of our Lord Jesus Christ. As I already stated, I believe that the main agenda behind the modern hybrid program (that has now already been going on for decades) is the creation of the antichrist and the false prophet. Doug Riggs, whom I believe to be an authority on the issue, believes that the first Nephilim of the modern era was born in 1962—50 years ago. In this way, it is not too much of a stretch to presume that the antichrist and false prophet may already be waiting in the wings, awaiting the moment of their apocalypse (unveiling) on the earth.

Agenda #2—Transhumanism

Upon reading chapter eight (Eugenics), the reader may have noticed that I often mentioned technocracy. Though the idea of elites using technology to achieve social control is a theme in that chapter, the reader may have felt that I had failed to connect a couple of dots. If you felt this way, you were right! From eugenics and Darwinism, to Planned Parenthood and the Third Reich, to genetics and environmentalism, there is a common thread. But this thread doesn't end with the enviro-whackoism of the militant green movement. It all dovetails in Transhumanism.

Now, Transhumanism is not an issue that is likely at the forefront of your average Christian's thinking. Many Christians may not even know exactly what I am talking about when I use the term Transhumanism. With that in mind, I came up with the following working definition of Transhumanism:

> "A genetic revolution that seeks to enhance the human species through managed evolution, by way of genetic engineering, mind sciences, and the manipulation of matter, for the express purpose of creating a post-human race."

Notice the presuppositions of Social Darwinism and how this parallels the concepts of eugenics (selective breeding). I interviewed Canadian researcher Carl Teichrib in 2011, and he told me concerning Transhumanism and its evolutionary assumptions:

> "When we have a belief in evolution, we can therefore take this technology and mankind can squeeze the evolutionary process and create man in our own image. . . . [In Transhumanism] this concept constantly emerges that through man's technology, through the works of our hands, man is able to transcend where we have come from and to move into a higher phase of evolution. Man will be the guiding influence. Man will play God."

Notice the blurring between the scientific and the religious realms taking place here. This is a key trend which the average person doesn't yet see coming. We also see the Enlightenment concept of the perfectibility of man coming into play here, which flies in the face of the Biblical concept of Original Sin. Man cannot only play God, he can *become* a god. Man can live forever! (If this sounds over the top, I just saw an article last week where a Russian scientist predicts that elites will be able to live forever by 2045.)

In Transhumanism, we see *the lie* that Satan told in the Garden of Eden:

1) You surely will not die
2) You will be like God

Transhumanism is also pluralistic, as Carl Teichrib told me:

> "Religions that hold to exclusive truth claims are non-participants in the global setting. Instead of

continuing to push the unity of man, they divide mankind. So we need a form of spirituality that will unite, that will harmonize, and that will bring together the world. It will be an evolving spirituality—one that can take all the best elements out of all the various faiths."

Again, this is not purely scientific. There is a mystical side to Transhumanism. Carl further stated:

"Some people will look back and say that Transhumanism is working toward the Nietzsche idea of superman. And that's partially right, and it's also partially wrong. Where it really is more moving towards is the idea of Chardin's *The Future of Man* —man evolving, not just biologically but man evolving spiritually, man evolving mystically."

Gary Kah writes in *The New World Religion* that "[Pierre Teilhard de Chardin's] concepts and teachings run like a continuous thread through the tapestry of New Age spirituality."[19] Gary further writes:

"As a Jesuit priest, Teilhard would always pursue his first love, which was the blending of the physical and spiritual worlds under the banner of evolution."[20]

Chardin taught that mankind is evolving towards an omega point (a quantum leap), at which time transcendent humanity will be united spiritually. Brzezinski's *Technotronic Era,* Al Gore's environmentalism, and Robert Muller's

Worldcore Curriculum all show the fingerprints of Chardin's influence.

I have interviewed Gary Kah several times over the past few years. In one 2011 interview Gary told me:

> "In order to have a true new world order, global government, you need to have not only an economic and political global system, you need to have a coming together of the world's religions to make such a system possible. Without this type of unity or at least a semblance of unity, you can't really have a world system. And the people that are pushing for a new world system, a one world system, understand that. And so religion has been a big part of the equation for a long time. . . . It's all headed towards global unity under the antichrist and under the coming world system."

Having looked at the philosophical side of Transhumanism, there are also technological considerations. The world is already wrestling with the emergence of new sciences like nanotechnology, information technology, biotechnology, and cognitive science. A British lab has already admitted to creating 150 human-animal chimeras. Scientists can already interface the human brain with computers and it is theoretically possible to create designer babies and super soldiers. (I am certain that the latter has already occurred.) Technocrats are already talking about downloading a person's essence (like software) before they die so that when technology catches up at a later date they will be able to install the software into some sort of humanoid hardware. These capabilities, needless to say, create profound ethical and moral questions (as Brzezinski observed).

Is Transhumanism the ultimate utopian carrot, as Carl Teichrib asked me? If so, it is worth noting that supposedly utopian societies don't have a history of ending well. From the blood bath of the French Revolution, the Russian Revolution, the Third Reich, and beyond, utopianist visions have a way of ending with the shedding of much blood. Is it not conceivable that DARPA, NASA, Monsanto, and other entities, once they are in possession of powerful new technologies, could drop the hammer and enslave a helpless humanity? Are "offworld" intelligences already working with black programs that operate at security classifications well beyond top secret (like cosmic)?

I believe that the origin of much of our modern day technology is supernatural. While I'm not certain that I can offer smoking-gun evidence, I believe a bargain has been made between the kings of the earth and Satan's hierarchy of evil. In exchange for the women (to be used in the breeding/genetic engineering program), supernatural technology has been given—for example antigravity propulsion. This bargain sheds light as to how and why major corporations and governments like North Korea and the UN engage in human trafficking, white slavery, and child pedophile rings. Within this labyrinth of evil is a nightmarish netherworld of Satanic Ritual Abuse, Dissociative Identity Disorder, Monarch Programming and MK-Ultra experiments—all of which in varying ways help to conceal these horrendous programs and their true Satanic agenda.

Fourth Reich and the Mark

After World War II, many of the scientists of the Third Reich evaded Nuremberg by disappearing into North and

South America by way of the Vatican ratlines and Operation Paperclip—coordinated by elements of American intelligence. The Nazi scientists (who were also occult adepts) were quickly and secretly recruited by the governments of the world who sought to benefit from their technologies and methodologies. I have personally interviewed Doug Riggs, who has counseled victims of Satanic Ritual Abuse for decades. Unbelieveable as it may sound, Doug has worked with individuals who have been Satanically programmed by Dr. Joseph Mengele himself. Through horrific chronic early childhood trauma, programmers push the victim until his personality splits. The split is a defense mechanism which, through dissociation, helps the victim cope with the severe trauma he is experiencing. (Examples include rape and occultic sex rituals, intentional drowning and resuscitation, being buried alive, etc.). Drugs are also used in the shaping process. When the split occurs, the programmer basically has raw personality material that he can then shape the way he wants. Occult rituals are often performed in which the programmer literally acts as a sorcerer to channel in demonic spirits. Through these spirits, superhuman abilities can be created (reconnaissance abilities, telepathy, ability to speak ancient dead languages, super-human strength, etc.). Not surprisingly, when these Satanic sleepers become adults they are placed in the military, intelligence, law enforcement, and especially the remnant Church—which poses the greatest potential threat of revealing and opposing Satan's last days agenda of deception and global dominance under the coming antichrist. (Note: we are not even dealing here with hybrids and genetic modification, these are merely capabilities that are engineered through Satanic programming.) Russ Dizdar's book *The Black Awak-*

ening deals with how literally an army of Satanic sleepers are programmed to, on the day of activation, overthrow the United States and Western governments for the specific purpose of creating the chaos from which the antichrist will emerge as world leader. While the *sleepers* are charged with orchestrating the chaos, Doug Riggs asserts that the *hybrids* will serve as the armies of antichrist once he has ascended to power. In other words, the hybrids will essentially serve as the SS Officers of the Fourth Reich.

One well-known characteristic of the dissociative splits that occur during Satanic programming is amnesia. In this way a person can be programmed and not even be aware of it. A skilled programmer can literally create layers (other alter personalities) which serve as protective barriers guarding the deepest levels of dissociation. The deepest, most secretive aspects of the Luciferian agenda are concealed, of course, within these deepest layers. Doug Riggs, observing from decades of experience, says that the Nephilim/hybrid program is the unholy grail that lurks behind the darkest and most secretive aspects of Satanic Ritual Abuse and Dissociative Identity Disorder. The women-for-technology paradigm leads inevitably to this labyrinth of unadulterated radical evil.

Just in my own lifetime (I'm 32), the increase in technology has been breathtaking. The frenetic pace will only increase. As a matter of fact, I believe technology has been actively suppressed to the point that what the general public sees as the latest and greatest is at least two or three decades behind what actually exists. (I believe this figure could be quite conservative.) My conjecture is that, about the time the "alien" disclosure is made, much of the suppressed technology will be released. This will have the effect of creating a fake evolutionary quantum leap, both technologically and spiritually. It will be an unprecedented propaganda assault on humanity, who, through the media and education, have already been pre-programmed and conditioned to accept that which is coming. The deception will be so powerful and so overwhelming that even the few who actually understand what has happened will feel themselves being seduced by what Johanna Michaelsen calls the beautiful side of evil.

On top of all of this, I believe that the Mark of the Beast will be a genetic source code (with RFID characteristics) that will literally offer humanity the "opportunity" to become god-like through genetic enhancement. L. A. Marzulli pioneered this view in his important book, *Cosmic Chess Match*, which is based on more than mere speculation but on actual field research. Marzulli examined the work of Dr. Roger Leir who conducted experiments on actual implants removed from 'alien' abductee victims, which led Marzulli to connect the dots between the so-called Mark of the Beast and Revelation.[21] Revelation 9:6, which reads:

> *"And in those days men will seek death and will not find it; they will long to die, and death flees from them."* [22]

Why is it that men will seek to die but will not be able to? In light of the technological and spiritual ramifications of Transhumanism, it no longer seems unthinkable that Satan will be able to deliver the goods in terms of life extension and even eternal life. (You will not surely die.)

But what a trap this is! A good theological definition for death is simply separation. By permitting death, God has actually graciously provided a way whereby humanity can be reunited to Him (through the blood of Christ). But if we achieve immortality in our state of sin, then logically we have prevented ourselves from even having the possibility of being reconciled to God.

Furthermore, we are told in Revelation 14:9-11 that anyone who takes the Mark of the Beast is damned and that their judgment is irrevocable. Again I ask, is there something about the Mark of the Beast that so alters human DNA that those who accept it are no longer considered 'human enough' to be able to receive the free gift of salvation through our Lord Jesus Christ? The text certainly appears to allow for this possibility. This appears to be the true agenda behind Transhumanism.

I am sensitive to the fact that many readers will not be able to process the existence of such radical evil. I understand the urge to not want to believe these things. I know these realities can be unsettling and uncomfortable (to say the least). However, as C. S. Lewis wrote in *Mere Christianity*, comfort is not my main concern:

> "If you look for truth, you may find comfort in the end: if you look for comfort you will not get either comfort or truth."(23)

My comfort in unearthing these soiled realities has been a bigger view of God. If the evil is this profound and the darkness this oppressive, how much bigger must our infinitely good God be? The world has gone wrong, but at the end of history it will all be righted. As C. S. Lewis said, we live in the part of the universe occupied by the enemy. That's why the Bible teaches that the whole world lies under the power of the evil one—whom Jesus called the god of this world. The evil one *blinds the minds of the unbelieving so that they might not see the light of the gospel of the glory of Christ, who is the image of God* (2 Corinthians 4:4). The evilness of evil only points back to the goodness of good.

This book has dealt with some of the tactics I believe the enemy employs to "do the blinding." However, at the end of the day I realize that the Truth of the Gospel is spiritually discerned and that it is not my place or role to do the convincing. That task is the work of the Holy Spirit. As we rapidly plunge headlong into the last of the last days, the choice will becoming increasingly clear. Jesus or Satan. Good or evil. Those who, in the name of temporary comfort, choose to side with evil should consider the second Psalm:

> *Why are the nations in an uproar*
> *And the peoples devising a vain thing?*
> *The kings of the earth take their stand*
> *And the rulers take counsel together*
> *Against the Lord and against His Anointed, saying,*
> *Let us tear their fetters apart*
> *And cast away their cords from us!*
> *He who sits in the heavens laughs,*
> *The Lord scoffs at them.*
> *Then He will speak to them in His anger*
> *And terrify them in His fury, saying,*
> *"But as for Me, I have installed my King*
> *Upon Zion, My holy mountain."*
>
> *"I will surely tell of the decree of the Lord:*
> *He said to Me, 'You are my Son,*
> *Today I have begotten You.*
> *Ask of Me, and I will surely give the*

nations as Your inheritance,
And the very ends of the earth as Your possession.
You shall break them with a rod of iron,
You shall shatter them like earthenware.' "

Now therefore, O kings, show discernment;
Take warning, O judges of the earth.
Worship the Lord with reverence
And rejoice with trembling.
Do homage to the Son, that He not become angry,
and you perish in the way,
For His wrath may soon be kindled.
How blessed are all who take refuge in Him!

The Luciferian doctrine is that those serving Satan can somehow derail the second coming and thus somehow avert the inevitable judgment that is coming. This delusional hubris is laughable. In a matter of moments the Lord Jesus will defeat the forces of antichrist who have gathered at Armageddon to combat Him and the armies of heaven (Psalm 2). By the Word of His mouth and the brightness of His coming the nations will be subdued and the kings of the earth will be annihilated.

We are facing a global economic collapse, including the implosion of the Euro and the American dollar. World events are rapidly moving towards World War III, which will most likely involve the use of thermonuclear weapons. Damascus will be destroyed, as will probably Rome. The United States could descend into civil war with the police state eventually dropping the hammer as martial law is declared. Global famine and pestilences will occur and volcanoes will violently come to life. Islands will disappear into the sea like Atlantis as powerful mega-quakes rock the planet. Those who survive will face unprecedented supernatural manifestations as the veil between the spiritual and the temporal realms is significantly compromised or altogether breached. Breath-taking technologies will be released as a pretext for claiming that a quantum leap in human evolution has finally arrived. Christians will be persecuted as a pluralistic, inclusive planetary spirituality takes hold of the world.

Regardless of one's eschatological orientation, it is foolish to assume that the Church will not go through a difficult trial. As to preparing for the coming chaos by stocking up on food, water, medicine, gold, silver, and supplies, I am not in a position to give the reader advice (as everybody's situation is different). I can only say seek the Lord's guidance and walk with Him in an intimate way every day. Be filled with the Holy Spirit and continually nourish yourself with the Word of God. Begin to engage in advanced Spiritual warfare and find rest in the secret place.

The good news is that out of this trial I believe the Church will see its finest hour. The day will come when it will be obvious who the true Christians are as we will see exploits that will outstrip even the Book of Acts. The Holy Spirit will empower us to overcome our fears as we boldly proclaim the Truth of the Gospel to anyone who will listen. We know that if we endure to the end we will be overcomers and that the temporary troubles of this world will be swallowed up by the glories and blessings of Heaven and the Millennial Kingdom that await us. This will not be a time to cower in fear, but a time to stand up boldly in the face of the evil day knowing that greater is He who is within us than he who is in the world. Godspeed, brothers and sisters.

Now it's time to add the final items to *The Omega Manifesto*:

36) The angel-human hybrid/genetic engineering program of Genesis 6 is occurring again in our day.
37) The purpose of that program is to produce antichrist (and the false prophet) who will be the primary DNA source code for both the mark and the image of the beast (Revelation 13:11-18).
38) Disclosure of off-world life is imminent and the hybrid races that will be revealed will include the armies of antichrist.
39) Luciferian Transhumanism will also produce the Mark of the Beast, which it seems will be a transgenic source code with RFID characteristics. Through the Mark the original lie from the Garden of Eden will be retold: you will not surely die and you will be as gods.
40) After the the dust settles from the coming mass chaos and when the radical paradigm transformation isfinally complete, humanity's choice will be simple: Jesus Christ or Satan. Good or Evil. Heaven or Hell.

Chapter 10 Endnotes

(1) http://www.blueletterbible.org/cgi-bin/words.pl?book= Deu&chapter=32&verse=22&strongs=07585&page=1&flag_full=1

(2) www.carm.org/dictionary/dic_g-h.htm

(3) Strong's 5020 (Greek).

(4) Tom Horn, *Nephilim Stargates*, 27.

(5) Chuck Missler and Mark Eastman, *Alien Encounters*, 36-37.

(6) Ibid., 208.

(7) Ibid.

(8) Horn, *Nephilim Stargates*, 94.

(9) Missler and Eastman, 224.

(10) Ibid., 96.

(11) Ibid, 79.

(12) Ibid., 67.

(13) Ibid., 120.

(14) John Ankerberg and John Weldon *The Facts on UFOs and Other Supernatural Phenomena*, 13.

(15) Tom Horn, *Apollyon Rising*, 91.

(16) Missler and Eastman quoting Bud Hopkins, *Witnessed*, 378.

(17) Missler and Eastman quoting Dr. O'Leary at the 1994 International Forum on New Science (Ft. Collins, CO).

(18) www.newswithviews.com/Horn/thomas155.htm#_ftn1

(19) Gary Kah, *The New World Religion*, 62-63.

(20) Ibid., 63

(21) L. A. Marzulli, *Cosmic Chess Match*, 269.

(22) Ibid, 271-273.

(23) C. S. Lewis, *Mere Christianity*, 32.

The Omega Manifesto

1) Truth exists.
2) Truth is knowable.
3) Approach Truth Didactically (antithesis), not Dialectically (synthesis).
4) Natural Law exists (intrinsic human morality).
5) A Lawgiver exists behind Natural Law (the Triune first cause).
6) The incredible design of the universe points to the Designer.
7) Everything in the universe is not presently as it ought to be.
8) The Bible indicates that the earth, in its present form, is 6,000 to 10,000 years old.
9) The creation Adam and Eve enjoyed was originally perfect.
10) Sin and death entered through Adam, not through evolution that took place over the course of untold geological ages.
11) Gap Theory, so long as it does not contradict items 9 and 10, is an acceptable position to take.
12) A Didactic approach to Truth does not ensure that one actually possesses Truth. Didactic bullies and Truth trolls serve as small-minded examples of this fact.
13) The present world order will not continue indefinitely. Christ is coming back again.
14) We appear to be in the general time and season of Christ's second coming.

15) Before Christ's second coming, the New World Order will present a false Messiah who will enter into a seven year covenant with many, including Israel.

16) We must resist and expose tyranny and the New World Order so long as we have life in our bodies.

17) God unilaterally and unconditionally instituted the Abrahamic Covenant.

18) The Law of Moses (The Mosaic Covenant) was an imperfect and temporary covenant which pointed forward to Christ and the New Covenant.

19) Like the Mosaic Covenant, the New Covenant is to be seen within the broader context of the Abrahamic Covenant—the implication being that the New Covenant in no way replaces the Abrahamic Covenant.

20) The existence of the modern state of Israel is prophetically significant and points forward to the fulfillment of Daniel's 70th Week (a seven year period).

21) The Church does not replace Israel in God's plan for man.

22) The Church has sinned against Israel and the Jewish people throughout its history—the Body of Christ must repent if she is to avoid committing the same sins again in the future.

23) There is nothing new about the New World Order, which goes all the way back to the political and religious system of ancient Babel.

24) The mystical essence of that system was preserved in the Mystery Religions and occult secret societies down through the ages.

25) The Illuminati are those who are consciously working on behalf of Lucifer to bring about global government and a one world religion that will serve Satan's false messiah.

26) The Federal Reserve system is the economic mechanism that has been used in America and around the world to build the New World Order.

27) The same powers behind the Fed set up the CFR which is the establishment / shadow government in America. These same people created the United Nations, the Bilderberg Group, and the Trilateral Commission, which are all working in tandem to moveus towards World Government.

28) While establishing structures that will lead to global economic and political integration, the NWO has engaged in a subversive cultural revolution using education and the media to re-program the public.

29) The False Flag is a go-to play in the globalist playbook.

30) A coming financial storm (of which 2008 was only an appetizer) will be the mother of all false flags and will signal the final take down of America and the West and emergence of a truly global government.

31) The crack-pot science of modern day radical environmentalism is the present manifestation of the crack-pot science of eugenics.

32) If global elites have their way, the world population will be reduced from 7 billion to somewhere between 500 million and 2 billion.

33) The Emergent Church / Purpose Driven / Church Growth movements have brought the Dialectical process into the church and are to be renounced.

34) The Word of God, illuminated by the Holy Spirit, is our source of Absolute Truth. This is a non-negotiable.

35) Persecution is coming to the church in America and the West.

36) The angel-human hybrid / genetic engineering program of Genesis 6 is occurring again in our day.
37) The purpose of that program is to produce antichrist (and the false prophet) who will be the primary DNA source code for both the mark and the image of the beast (Revelation 13:11-18).
38) Disclosure of off-world life is imminent and the hybrid races that will be revealed will include the armies of antichrist.
39) Luciferian Transhumanism will also produce the Mark of the Beast, which it seems will be a transgenic source code with RFID characteristics. Through the Mark the original lie from the Garden of Eden will be retold: you will not surely die and you will be as gods.
40) After the the dust settles from the coming mass chaos and when the radical paradigm transformation isfinally complete, humanity's choice will be simple: Jesus Christ or Satan. Good or Evil. Heaven or Hell.

Index

-A-

Abomination of Desolation—55-57

Abrahamic Covenant—35, 67, 70, 72-75, 77, 78, 86, 95, 224

Absolute Truth—11, 13, 18-20, 24, 47, 70, 168, 169, 172, 174, 182, 225

Agenda 21—156-158, 163

Ahmadinejad, Mahmoud—92

Aldridge, Nelson—106

Alexander the Great—96

Allen, Gary—137

APEC—120

Aristotle—11, 12

Artaxerxes—50, 58

ASEAN—120

Augustine—82-84

-B-

Babylon Working—196

Bacon, Francis—102

Bell, Rob—170, 171, 179

Bernays, Edward—145, 146

Bilderberg—118, 119, 121, 140, 146, 225

Biometrics—142

Biotechnology—206, 207, 212

Blair, Tony—178, 179

Bolsheviks—112, 115

Book of Enoch—192

Book of Jasher—195

Book of Jubilees—193, 205, 206

BP—132
Brzezinski, Zbigniew—119, 149, 150, 211, 212
Bullinger, E. W.—89, 90

-C-
Carbon Taxes—120
Carnegie Institute—143
Carter, Jimmy—149
CFR—(see Council on Foreign Relations)
Chase Bank—138, 144
Cheney, Dick—134
Chesteron, G.. K.—25, 30, 59
Churchill, Winston—115
CIA—123, 132, 133
Clement of Alexandria—194
Club of Rome—149
Coal and Steel Community—118, 119
Cold Spring Harbor Laboratory—143
Cosmological Argument—26
Council on Foreign Relations—105, 113-116, 119, 122, 130,
    140, 147, 178, 225
Crowley, Aleister—122-124, 195, 196
Crusades—83, 91, 100
Crysostom, John—83
Cuddy, Dennis—125, 126

-D-
Dallas Theological Seminary—89
Daniel's 70th Week—54, 56, 58, 64, 75, 95, 224
Dante—14, 191
DARPA—213
Darwin, Charles—142, 145
Darwinism—25, 142, 144, 154, 157, 209
Da Vinci, Leonardo—13, 14

Day Age Theory—37
Dead Sea Scrolls194
Demoralization—47
Department of Education—125, 128
Department of Homeland Security—135, 139
Dewey, John—125, 126, 146
DHS (see Department of Homeland Security)
DID (see Dissociative Identity Disorder)
Dialectic (see Hegelian Dialectic)
Diaspora—53, 87, 88
Didactic Thought—11, 13, 15, 18, 19, 44-46, 170, 223
Dissociative Identity Disorder—213, 215
Dizdar, Russ—5, 214
DNA—26, 27, 204, 206, 217, 221, 226
Drucker, Peter—172-175, 177
Dulles, Allen—132
DuPont—144

-E-
Enlightenment—13, 14, 18, 112, 210
Epistemology—9, 11
Euro—119, 219
European Economic Community—119
European Union—119, 120
Evolution—23, 25, 31, 32, 27, 46, 159, 209-211, 220, 223
Existentialism—17, 23, 24

-F-
Fabian Socialists—113, 115, 125, 167
False Flag—131, 134, 136, 140, 225
F. D. R. (see Roosevelt, Franklin D.)
Fed, The (see Federal Reserve)
Federal Reserve—105, 106, 109-113, 115, 136, 139, 140, 225
FEMA—135, 139

Flynn, David—45
Ford Foundation—118, 155
Ford Motor Company—144, 148
Fourth Reich—213, 215
Freemasonry—101-103, 115, 178
French Revolution—13, 14, 213
Freud, Sigmund—145
Fuller Theological Seminary—177

-G-
Galton, Francis—142-145
Galton Institute—159
Gap Theory—40-42, 44-46, 198, 199, 223
Gates, Bill—159
GATT—119
General Motors—144
Giants—193, 195, 204
Gingrich, Newt—179
Glass-Owen Bill—109
Glass-Steagall—138
Gnosticism—97, 100, 102
Gorbachev, Mikhail—168
Gore, Al—119, 120, 154, 211
Grand Orient Lodge—103
Great Depression—110, 115
Griffin, G. Edward—105, 106, 108, 110, 115
Gulf Oil—133
Gulf of Tonkin—133

-H-
Hades—188-191, 208
Ham, Ken—31, 32, 45
Hay, Harry—123, 124
Hegel, G. W. F.—14-18

Hegelian Dialectic—16-19, 25, 45, 113, 117, 128, 130, 157, 168, 170-172, 174, 177, 178, 181, 223, 225

Hinduism—99

Hitler, Adolf—23, 82, 83, 92, 98, 115, 173

Holdren, John—153-155

Holocaust—82, 83, 92, 93

Horn, Tom—5, 102, 194, 200, 201, 205

Horus—123

Hubbard, L. Ron—195

Humanist Manifesto—125, 126

Hussein, Saddam—92

Huxley, Aldous—146, 149, 171

Huxley, Julian—128, 144, 146, 159

Hybels, Bill—179, 181

-I-

IBM—144

Illuminati—101, 103, 110, 224

IMF (See International Monetary Fund)

Industrial Revolution—112

Inquisitions——83, 93

International Monetary Fund—148

Irenaeus—194

Islam—80, 82, 90-92, 166, 171, 179

-J-

Jekyll Island—105, 106, 108, 109, 115

Jesuits—103, 104, 211

Jet Propulsion Laboratory—195

Johnson, Lyndon—133, 134, 148

Jones, Alex—131, 137, 139

Jones, Tony—170

Josephus—194

Justin Martyr—82, 194

-K-

Kabalah—100-102
Kah, Gary—5, 100, 104, 111, 115, 156, 165, 211, 212
Kaiser Wilhelm Institute—143
Kierkegaard, Soren—17, 18, 23, 24
Kinsey, Alfred—123, 124
Kissinger, Henry—150
Knights Templars—100-103
Koran—90, 91

-L-

L. B. J. (see Johnson, Lyndon)
Leap of Faith—17, 18
Leary, Timothy—123
Lewis, C .S.—21, 30, 31, 217
Loeffler, John—5, 14, 16, 23, 47, 113, 164, 165, 180
LSD—123
Luciferian—101, 102, 201, 215, 219, 226

-M-

MacDonald, George—33
Malthus, Thomas—142
Malthusian—142
Mark of the Beast—208, 216, 217, 221, 226
Marxism—16, 17, 19
Masonry—(see Freemasonry)
Mengele, Josef—144, 214
McLaren, Brian—170, 171, 179
McNamara, Robert—133, 147, 148
MI6—118, 132
Michelangelo—13, 14
Middle Ages—13, 14
Millennial Kingdom—63, 64, 208, 220
Milner Roundtable Groups—104, 114

Mind Control—123, 146, 150, 213-218
Missler, Dr. Chuck—5, 27, 38, 80, 83, 194, 196, 197, 207
MK-Ultra—123, 213
Monarch Programming—213
Monsanto—159, 213
Monteith, Dr. Stanley—5, 111, 122
Morgan, J. P.—105, 106, 113, 138
Moral Relativism—170
Mosaic Covenant—36, 62, 70-75, 86, 95, 224
Moses—35, 36, 52, 62, 64, 70, 71, 74, 95, 224
Mossadegh, Mohammad—132
Mount Hermon—199
Muller, Robert—128, 211
Mystery Religions—98-100, 102, 110, 224

-N-
NAFTA—119, 120, 158
NAFTA Superhighway—120, 158
Nanotechnology—27, 206, 207, 212
Napoleon—98, 131
NASA—213
NATO—133
Natural Law—21, 26, 29, 168, 174, 223
Nephilim—186, 187, 191-195, 203, 204, 207, 209, 215
Nero—131
New Age—123, 176, 177, 195, 200, 211
New Covenant—73-75, 95, 224
New World Order—55, 57, 59, 65, 97, 100, 101, 103, 110-113,
    117, 120, 125, 131, 140, 146, 151,164, 166, 167, 169, 179,
    198, 200, 201, 207, 212, 224, 225
NGO (see Non-Governmental Organizations)
Nimrod—66, 98, 99, 203, 205, 206
Nixon, Richard—136

Noah—34, 40, 61, 63, 66, 67, 98, 184-187, 191, 193, 195, 199, 200, 204-207
Non-Governmental Organizations—156, 168
North American Union—119, 120, 158
NSSM 200—150, 151

-O-
Obama, Barack—149, 153, 154, 167
Occult—99, 100, 102-104, 110, 124, 125, 176, 195, 200, 201, 206, 207, 214, 224
Operation Ajax—132
Operation Gladio—133
Operation Himmler—132
Ordo Templi Orientus—133
Origen—82
Original Sin—26, 210
Osiris—99
OTO (see Ordo Templi Orientus)

-P-
Passover—62, 63
Parsons, Jack—195
Patriot Act—132, 135
Pentecost, Dr. Dwight—89
Philo—194
Planned Parenthood—143, 151, 209
Plato—11, 12, 142
Pogroms—83, 93
Population Council—147
Potter, Charles Francis—125, 126
Prince Bernhard—118
Prince Philip—146, 155, 159

-Q-
Quayle, Steve—195

-R-
Ramadan—171
Reichstag—132
Relative Truth—16, 174
Renaissance—11, 13, 14, 18
Replacement Theology—78, 80-86, 90, 93-95
RFID—216, 221, 226
Rhodes, Cecil John—103, 104, 114
Rhodes Scholarships—104
Riggs, Doug—5, 206-208, 214, 215
Rio Earth Summit—156-168
Rockefeller Jr., David—119, 121
Rockefeller, John D.—105, 106, 116, 147, 178, 179
Rockefeller Foundation—114, 118, 123, 155
Rockefellers—105, 113, 125, 138, 143, 144, 146, 149, 178, 179
Roman Catholicism—102, 179
Roosevelt, Franklin D.—114, 115, 132, 133
Roosevelt, Kermit—132, 133
Rosicrucian—102
Rosslyn Chapel—102
Roswell—196
Rothschild, Nathan—131
Rothschilds—103-106, 113, 131, 138
Royal Dutch Shell—118, 154
Royal Institute of International Affairs—104, 114, 118
Russian Revolution—112, 213

-S-
Saddleback Church—173, 175
Sanger, Margaret—143
Satanic Ritual Abuse—213-215

Schaeffer, Francis—5, 14, 16, 18, 30, 47, 165, 169, 280
Scientology—195
Security and Prosperity Partnership—119, 120
Shinar—57, 192
Six Day War—133, 134
Skull and Bones—143
Speed of Light—38, 39
SRA (see Satanic Ritual Abuse)
Stalin, Joseph—173
Standard Oil—144

-T-
Tavistock Institute—123
Teichrib, Carl—5, 209, 210, 213
Teilhard de Chardin, Pierre—211
Tertullian—194
Theistic Evolution—37
Third Reich—132, 143, 144, 209, 2123
Titus—53, 62
Total Quality Management—172, 175
Tower of Babel—98, 99, 199
Transatlantic Economic Council—120
Transhumanism—209-213, 216, 217, 221, 226
Trans Texas Corridor—120
Trilateral Commission—118, 119, 140, 225
Turner, Ted—159

-U-
UFO—196-198, 200, 201
UN (see United Nations)
UNCED (see Rio Earth Summit)
UNESCO—128, 145, 146
UN Convention on Biodiversity—156, 158
Uniformity of Natural Causes—39

United Nations—62, 115, 116, 120, 127, 128, 140, 145, 147, 148, 151, 152, 154, 213, 225
Universal Truth—10, 11, 14, 16, 20
USS Liberty—133, 134
USSR—168, 169

-W-
Wall Street—105, 106, l09, 136-138, 167
Warburg, Paul—105, 113
Warren, Rick—172-179, 181
Watchers, The—192-194, 205, 206
Weishaupt, Adam—102-104
Wells, H. G.—144
Willow Creek—180
World Bank—147, 148
Worldcore Curriculum—212
World Council of Churches—179
World Wildlife Fund—118, 146, 147, 154
WWF (see World Wildlife Fund)

-Z-
Zacharias, Ravi—5, 23, 24, 26, 30, 32
Zionism—85
Zoroastrianism—99

About the Author

Journalist, Theologian, and Researcher Scott A. Keisler brings a unique perspective to the table. His written articles and multimedia content focus on shattering the false-reality matrix in which most people live. An Evangelical Christian, Scott is a published author whose articles have appeared in the Hope for the World quarterly newsletter, Collegehoopsnet.com, DaysofNoah.org, and ScottKeisler.com. Scott also edited the book *When the Cross Became a Sword* (Merrill Bolender), which has sold thousands of copies worldwide and has been translated into over a half-a-dozen languages.

Scott has a Master of Theological Studies from the Anderson University School of Theology and a BA in Journalism from Indiana University. As a webmaster, Scott's websites have achieved close to a quarter-million unique visitors in over 80 countries and territories around the world. His podcasts and YouTube videos have been viewed by thousands of social network users.